HEART ON BREAK

*Taking a break from relationships
to become a better man*

NAKADA

This is dedicated to men who want to lead compassionately, love unconditionally, and build healthy families and communities.

CONTENTS

Introduction 1

How Women See You & How You See Yourself............................. 6

Mr. Unemotional.. 14

Moving On When There Are Children Involved 27

Taking a Break From Relationships 42

Accountability & Moving On 61

Attract Your Type 73

Breaking Unhealthy Soul Ties 85

Committed to Healthy Living 92

Back on the Market After a Break 116

A Balanced Approach to Family 133

About the Author & Ways to Connect 154

INTRODUCTION

My primary goal with this book is to inspire men to take well-deserved breaks from relationships to focus on being an improved version of themselves. I'm talking to guys who don't want to be real about what they need to fix about themselves, yet are constantly jumping from relationship to relationship because they don't want to be alone or don't know how to say no to women. A lot of us never underwent any sustained period of refinement that forced us to become better men. But like fine gold, you must go through the hottest fire to burn away all the impurities that we've collected from the world. When it comes to the relationship with the woman who will love you unconditionally as you strive towards your purpose in life, please believe that you just won't find her anywhere. So while you're on a break taking care of yourself, you won't miss out on her. I promise you that! Chances are she's waiting for you. You perhaps never found her because you've always been way too caught up with fly-by-night women who don't mean anything to you. This book calls into remembrance the lessons you've learned and the ones you ignored, too. The main focal point here isn't about the women, but rather about the self-work every man must do to dedicate himself to his life's calling. It's time to stop dating dead end women; stop going back and forth to dysfunctional relationships, and stop thinking that it's just sex because it's not.

I've always had a vision of the life I desired for myself and my family. But I haven't always done the required work to accomplish the goals needed to make my vision a reality. Self-doubt, lack of confidence, fear, and lack of discipline are all dream killers that I've experienced. What's worse, though, is when you're struggling on your path, but are nonetheless entertaining women who are draining you of your resources—mentally, physically, emotionally, financially and sexually. Where we get caught up the most is with sex. Whenever we finally find someone who fulfills our sexual desires, it's hard to throw all the sexual chemistry away, even if it's a dead end relationship. Many men enjoy the explosive sexual chemistry with the wrong women because of how alive they feel when the sex is that good—it's too easy to get stuck there without knowing that you're caught up. As I reflect upon my strongest unhealthy soul tie triggered by sex, I always knew that I couldn't tell her no long enough to avoid us having sex again and re-intensifying our soul tie. She knew she wasn't the one for me but figured that if she kept me coming, then I would be too caught up to go after the woman I was actually meant to be with. She knew I wasn't the one for her, but she was nonetheless not ready to let go of me. I must admit, though, keeping me coming almost worked because for a while I was very caught up in the sex. As caught up as I ever became in situations like these, I've always known better than to think sex defines a relationship—no matter how much fairy dust I was snorting.

Many of today's relationship experts aim their messages at women because marketing 101 says that women are more likely to buy their new book or watch their new TV show than men are. That might be true, but men are seeking to also find solutions to their personal and relational issues. Men must stop pointing the finger at women, become accountable for their actions and begin the path to finding the resources, encouragement, and support they need to help them grow—such as books like this. I talk a lot about accountability in this book because I believe that's what will help you on your path to change. If a man is avoiding being accountable, it's almost like he's saying he's unblemished and has done nothing wrong.

Accountability starts within you. If a man can't be accountable to accomplish his own life's mission, then why should he be relied upon for anything else? When you become accountable for your actions and its impact on others, then you finally have a chance to experience humility. With humility, you can clear your space of the negative energies of laziness, lack of discipline, overly stimulated sexuality, the ego and the women these low vibrational energies attracted to you. Taking this break from relationships is life or death for some men. Many of us have these addictions to temporary or dysfunctional relationships in common, and I know this to be true. I speak the truth about this because I've been a victim of my own good fortune with women. Even on a break, it's hard to avoid meeting new women or entertaining old flames. But the time alone is very necessary.

Men carry their pain in different ways. One of those ways is to mask it in their masculinity. That's a trend that has been constantly reinforced by today's media influences. Take note of how many young men are dying to become athletes, musicians, and superstars. It's not just for a scholarship or a career as a pro athlete. A lot of times it helps them disguise the pain of broken homes, sexual abuse, abusive parent(s), abandonment, coming from a rough environment, low self-esteem, lack of self-confidence, and the list goes on. Something like six percent become paid professional athletes. Another small percentage manage to get an education and some good life experiences out of it, but the mass majority end up stuck with the problems they've been hiding that soon overtake their lives when they're no longer in the spotlight. Then after all that disappointment of not making it to the top or even worse, getting there and not being able to stay there, here comes the women who are destined to make you feel better about yourself while in your broken stage. If a man can somehow recognize when he's at this stage of his life and stop to take the time to focus on his healing, I guarantee you that this world will be a better place. If the protectors and leaders are wounded, then everyone is at risk so the healing of the broken man is important for society at large.

The truth is that the woman for a man with dreams and visions is a rare gem. And this has been affirmed to me on the break I took from relationships to write this book. I'm not status quo. I don't want what everyone else wants. I don't like working for people, and there's no telling when I'm going to disappear into the bush somewhere. I already know that the average woman thinks I'm out of my damn mind. I know because they've been telling me for the last ten-plus years. On my break, I decided that I wouldn't let the nice assets and pretty smile of a beautiful stranger reel me in when I should be focused on manifesting my life's greatest work. I'd stay strong, smile, do a little closed end flirting, and keep it moving because we're not two peas in the same pod, and I know it. If you're not determined and are a bit more complacent, you can find yourself enjoying the distractions that come with relationships. These distractions are the type that leave many men with unfulfilled dreams and visions that they got too caught up to pursue.

These days, I end up turning down 100% of what's being offered to me because I literally can't afford to get caught up again in the stress of being with someone who is headed in an entirely different direction than I am. During my break, I ended up with my dick in my hand instead of between the legs of women who were giving me the green light. I love the attention I get from them, though, but I can see clearly now how falling for the feminine charm can sidetrack you from working diligently towards your goals. Taking note of the opportunities that come up and passing on them to remain focused will give you an opportunity to see how the women who come will be more and more ideal for you. When you're ready to date again it will require less of your time and you'll do it consciously in pursuit of an attractive woman who complements your lifestyle and is easy to give your love and protection to.

This break and the celibacy that came with it has taught me so much about valuing myself that I really wouldn't have it any other way. No one ever taught me that women would want sex from me just as much and sometimes more than I wanted it from them. No one ever said to me that too much sex with a woman who isn't the one would create an unhealthy soul tie. I'm 100% in this whole book. But it's not a sob story of my screw-ups with women. Every dysfunctional relationship cost me time and energy that I see now could've been well placed towards accomplishing my dreams. The break I speak of in this book is about valuing who you are and who you're becoming first, so when you do find the right woman, it's obvious to her that you value yourself. That sets the tone and creates the standard we must uphold for ourselves.

This book speaks to your ability to improve yourself holistically, strengthen your weaknesses and the importance of finding yourself before you go looking for love. There are those rare cases where a couple can find themselves together, but mostly people end up going in different directions once they begin to search for themselves. This book is about taking that time to do so and engaging in activities that help you center yourself so you can live the life that you were destined to live. That life would be a purpose driven one that requires you to stop all the distractions that women bring with them to get yourself more aligned with living in your purpose. Purpose isn't about achievement, but more about a lifestyle. You must never settle for a life you don't want to live, and this includes not settling with a woman who is not the right fit for you. Don't settle for her because she's the mother of your child. Don't settle because she's your first love or your high school sweetheart. The work that you do on yourself will eventually drive you into the arms of someone who will appreciate that you took the time to better yourself. That woman gets to be with a man who has ascended, instead of one who has fallen and can't get up. Men have one option: know yourself and live every day with purpose or remain dysfunctional and face becoming obsolete.

HOW WOMEN SEE YOU &
HOW YOU SEE YOURSELF

A LOT OF MEN END up viewing themselves based on how the women of our lives view us. Sometimes that starts with your mother and what she told you as a boy growing up. A lot of us were fed how handsome we were and how we were God's gift to the girls by our moms. For some boys, that can be enough to boost his confidence well into his teenage years and beyond. But not everyone grew up hearing positive things about himself as a boy from his mother or father. Sometimes the environment we came from was so harsh that very few positive and affirming words were ever said. In cases like these, the words needed to build confidence and self-esteem were few and far between while criticism and negativity were available in abundance.

You can run, but you really can't hide from your upbringing. , Your home environment tells an often forgotten story about how you view yourself and what you're accustomed to hearing about yourself. It's important to recognize when you need to work to repair negative thought patterns. Ultimately, you're going to have to strip yourself of all of the self-defeating ideals that were fed to you and begin to redefine yourself according to who you truly are. This is why men must take time away from relationships to find themselves and their purpose.

Women will admire a man for whatever they've been influenced to like men for. They can be attracted to you because of your physical appearance, your status, your material possessions, your intellect, etc. When you're young, and you don't know any better, to be admired by the one you want to be admired by is the greatest feeling in the world.

It's like a chemical high! It feels good and triggers so many different feelings within the body. If women liked you because you're tall, dark and handsome, you should take that to the bank. Whatever is your attraction point to women, use it wisely. I can't blame anyone for that. But the goal is to be confident in who you are and not allow women to shape your concept of self-worth. If the way you view yourself has been shaped by others, it's time to get your sculpting tool out to create a new image for yourself.

We now live in a culture where we see women on TV who are all made up from a number of cosmetic surgery augmentations. Men are being influenced to desire women who look like those women and not real ones. Now everyday women, in hopes of finding someone, are aiming to look like the fake ones they see on reality shows. I know firsthand because an ex of mine who couldn't control her fork decided to go under the knife to get closer to the Housewives of Atlanta look. She said it was for her, but I knew that it was an irresistible taste of superficiality that she thought would somehow make her more attractive and boost her self-esteem. There was no talking her out of it, but as I looked at all the superficiality she watched on TV, it became increasingly obvious that it had a huge influence on her if she felt she had to go to extremes to lose weight and look good. It made me wonder whether I was superficial, too. At first, I thought no, but then I learned the concept of how the partner we end up with is also a reflection of us. I attracted her to me based on some superficiality within me that I hadn't quite dealt with.

Reasons like those I have mentioned are why you need to understand a woman's value position before you get too caught up in all the nice things she has to say about you. With this same woman (who had the surgery), I had an on and off relationship, where she was the nicest and sweetest person I knew when she wanted intimacy with me. She would tell me everything I liked to hear when she wanted me. There was a time when I fell for it every single time—like clockwork! She was like the perfect girl, with all the right words when she wanted sexual intimacy from me. I always knew that it was just for the sex, but

7

I was in a vulnerable state in my life where I fell off and really wasn't dating at all. So every time she'd come back in the picture, I'd entertain her because I hadn't really put myself out there to pursue anyone else, and I felt I needed to blow some steam off with a good round of sex. Even though I never wanted to be with her, she was just so darn nice to me when we were sexually involved that I'd forget how superficial her need for me was. It was such an ego boost to know she wanted me that bad, whether or not it was for all the wrong reasons.

HOW YOU PRESENT YOURSELF

If you're the type of guy a lot of women are interested in, you must learn how to filter them out. If you're not that guy, and women aren't giving you buying signals, then you need to know why they're not interested in you. That's all part of your value proposition. It's important to know that when women are very interested in you, it could be a trap if you don't understand why they're interested in you in the first place. Women will throw themselves at you for artificial reasons sometimes, but they'll also stay away from you for artificial reasons as well. When women are constantly giving you the green light, it gets a little tricky on who to give attention to. Your time is valuable and ideally speaking, from this point out, you should never spend time on women who you can't develop feelings for. When you get smart about who to give your energy to, you'll eventually learn right away who's a waste of time. Unfortunately, it's going to be a lot of women who are beautiful but are not worth an ounce of your energy.

The truth is, women will see you how you present yourself, but if you lack confidence in who you are, they'll quickly choose to define you by whatever title fits you. During my professional photography days, I never wanted to be her photographer boy toy who a woman could easily seduce and walk away with $450 worth of services for free. Fall for this and it pretty much means you'll do anything to remain in their good graces. These kind of women are masters of building men up for the purpose of getting what they want. If your confidence is not strong, you'll be dependent on what these kinds of women have to say about you in order to build your self-confidence.

Your confidence in yourself has to be based on your true self-value. If a lot of women are interested in you, then you have options, and you'll walk with that confidence. If you're a good catch, you must behave like a good catch. If you're a good catch that doesn't behave like it, there'll come along a woman who plays the game very well, recognizes your lack of confidence in yourself and moves to use it to her advantage. If she's a pro, she'll have you wrapped around her fingers in no time and everything that makes you a good catch, she'll be sure to downplay to keep you worshipping her. Your lack of confidence in yourself can create these situations where you begin to behave how a woman programs you to behave. A buddy of mine fell victim to that a few times.

He was a great guy who treated women exceptionally well. In high school, we called him the "lover boy" because he didn't seem interested in pursuing multiple girls. He had been through a lot in his teenage years: both parents were missing from an early age, and later in life it became obvious that he really didn't have the tools at the time to develop a strong sense of self-value. Years later, he became absolutely a good catch: a nice guy with street smarts that women were interested in. But for a while, he was dependent on women to boost his confidence, and he'd try to overcompensate the women who made him feel really good about himself. Because he had this trait, it wasn't long before the wrong women took advantage of it. It took getting dragged through the mud by two different women before he realized his own self-worth. He'd eventually recognize some of the wrong moves he made with women that led him down roads he didn't want to be on. After he had taken a break, he came back with more self-confidence and was more assured of himself. He wasn't the guy in the room making all the noise, and he had learned to accept that about himself without feeling inadequate. He eventually learned that she who was right for him, wouldn't want him to change who he was for her to like him. He has since found a woman he can be loving and caring to who reciprocates that love to him without the need to take advantage of his tenderness. I'm happy for him because he grew to love himself more and didn't have to change his core beliefs to find love and happiness.

BUILD SELF-CONFIDENCE FROM WITHIN

No matter how much confidence you have in yourself, it's important not to get caught up in how a woman sees you, especially if you don't know what her values are. Let's face it—some women will want to have your babies because you're tall, muscular, rich, smart, dark skinned, light skinned or if you have blue eyes. All that shit is superficial! If you let these things boost your ego, and you begin to see yourself based on these things, then you just allowed someone else to build your self-confidence based on their ideals. You can't allow a shallow person to be the one who builds your confidence; you can't allow anyone at all to do that for you in your adult years. A shallow woman will soon enough drag you into the shallow end with her. Men do this to women all the time, too. You must build confidence yourself and base it on who you are and what you bring to the table—not the external or material things that you think women want. Some men just won't get to this level until they take a break from relationships and start analyzing all of their previous moves.

Many men have allowed their status and their material possessions to be what they build their self-image on. Whether it's the car, the outfit, the jewelry, the job, the house or whatever. Some men let it get to their heads and start believing that's who they really are. You have to be confident in your ability to execute and fulfill your desires in life, and that will always be an inside job that attracts women. This kind of confidence is what allows you to perform well on your job or your craft. Your ability to do the required things when necessary will be what people remember about you when there are no status symbols misrepresenting your image. Building self-confidence can certainly be done within a relationship, but if you find that this is just one of the many things you need to work on, then a break from relationships will give you that one-on-one time to help you rebuild your confidence in yourself to the point where you feel

100% assured of who you are and what you bring to the table when it comes to the woman you choose to be with.

Who the compliment is coming from is just as important as the compliment itself. It's nice to have a woman stroke your ego, but it's better to have someone who has some substance about herself complimenting you and encouraging you as you move forward. You'll value her input a lot more. You'll trust that what she expresses to you is heartfelt and genuine.

SHIELDING YOURSELF FROM THE NEGATIVITY AND TRICKERY

On the flip side of flattery, there'll be women who dislike you for one reason or the other; probably because you fucked them over. It's just as important, if not more important, not to get caught up in how they view you either. In this case, your growth as a man is what's more important because if there are women who hate your guts because of how you treated them, then they may have a legitimate reason for feeling that way. What's important when you're at this crossroad is to take accountability for the role you played in how she feels about you and walk tall in a different direction—one that's true to who you are and represents your new growth. If you cheated on her, abused her in any way, was dishonest to her or disenfranchised her, then you should understand why she feels the way she does. It doesn't mean you accept that as who you are, though, especially if you've made changes to be better. You don't have to be defined by your past, just do better and leave her the hell alone if you don't want to be with her.

It's important to know that embracing your wrongdoing in cases like these doesn't mean you become her whipping stick until she forgives you. What it means is that you choose to be humble because you know you have erred. Some women will hold a grudge forever, but you can't let that affect how you move on. You don't ever want to be in a position where you're trying to win her forgiveness. Nice guys fall for this shit all the time. I'm here to tell you—don't do it! She will take you for the ride of your life!

I found myself in that same position where my feeling of obligation had me trying to do things for her that she wasn't willing to do for herself. I didn't know what I was getting myself into, though. In these situations, expect that she'll play the victim role as long as you're willing to be the hero who swoops in to show her how sorry you are. She'll accept all that you're willing to offer as long as it puts her in a better position. It's really an ego boost for her to say look how you treated her in the past and look how you're bending over backward for her now. Any relationship built on obligatory actions rather than heartfelt actions is doomed. You both are really fooling yourselves in cases like these because you're only giving because you feel indebted to her while she reluctantly accepts with the mindset that you owe her, and she deserves to have you jumping through hoops for her. There's really no love here, and this woman is likely to never truly view you in the light that you want to be seen in. There might be some lingering love from your past relationship, but if your new situation is based on you earning her forgiveness, then you're being played.

The mistake you're making in a case like this is that your humility has failed. You probably had some time to reflect to yourself on how things went wrong, but quickly came running back to her trying to make things right (again). It's good when you've chosen to empathize with her hurt feelings, but you're seeking to change the way she views you by giving to her and simultaneously undervaluing yourself. You just won't get very far at all with this approach. As long as you continue to do this, you're viewing yourself the way she sees you—unworthy. She sees you as undeserving of her love, even if she was incapable of loving you in the first place. Her excuse for not truly loving you would sound more like, "you hurt me, and I need time." She will continue to hold her position as long as you also believe that you're responsible for all her pain and feed into her victimhood. If you're viewing yourself through her eyes, then you're agreeing to stay stuck in the past. If you constantly justify why you're willing to do so much for a woman who wouldn't do the same for you with the excuse of, "I do it because I did her wrong," then you're at risk of staying stuck in that role forever. You'll block your opportunity to become a better man if you consistently view yourself through the eyes of someone whose love for you is tainted by hurt and pain. Even if you caused it, mature and evolving people don't point fingers or hold grudges forever. You might have strong feelings for her or share a childwith her, but it's very important to distance yourself from this woman.

Whether it's the highest praises or the lowest insults, you can see why it's important that you not get caught up in how women see you. If her viewpoints can't help you get better as a man, then they're useless to you. Don't get caught up in who she is; learn to view things in black and white—it's either she's in support of you or she's against you. There's no in between. There'll be exes and for some, the mother(s) of your children, who will never be happy with you. You've got to learn to be happy regardless of how they feel about you—even when they refuse to stop talking trash about you. You must learn that you cannot carry her burden, even if your behavior has hurt her. Accountability and honesty are the gateways to making peace with women whose love for you has turned to bitterness, resentment, and hate. But understand that every woman who says that you've hurt her was not actually in love with you like she claims to have been. Sometimes all you hurt was their ego. For some women, the heartbreak happens when their expectations weren't met—that moment it became obvious to her that she was not going to look or feel how she envisioned it. Haven't we all had to endure through the disappointment of unmet expectations?

Humility is the key when dealing with the anguish or flattery of women of your past and present. You want to have a balanced approach to both situations—the flattery and the hate. When you are who you say you are, your life begins to happen how you think it will. If you spend too much time seeing yourself the way others view you, you'll never fully be you, and you'll be subject to the same unhappiness they suffer from because misery loves company.

MR. UNEMOTIONAL

I HAVE STRUGGLED WITH EXPRESSING my emotions in general, and that definitely has trickled off into my relationships. That's real life honesty that took me a long time to realize. I was engaged to the perfect woman, and it didn't occur to me until I broke off the engagement how little I expressed to her my deep sense of gratitude that God brought her into my life. From the moment I saw her, I longed for her. All that took was seeing her from across the room and not even uttering a word to her. I had a special connection with her that I never experienced before, but at the time, I just didn't know how to express that. She knew she was the one for me because she could read through my awkward attempts to tell her, but when I look back at how I expressed myself over four years together, I was dry on heartfelt words and outside of gifts and special occasions, I really didn't express to her how much I really loved her and how perfect I felt she was for me. With all the things I was pursuing in my life at the time, love wasn't one of them. Love was a byproduct of the relationship to me, but not my goal or what I was in pursuit of.

Many years later, I've been able to put a finger on that behavior in hopes of improving upon it. It's sad that it's literally taken me ten years to see how my lack of emotional expression has stunted my growth. I've since had two children with two different women, both from my past. Both relationships were terrible failures and I hold myself fully accountable for the role I've played in the failures. I was no doubt looking for love, but I wasn't being true to myself in the way I sought it. I see now how an outward expression of my desire for love and affection could've been the catalyst for receiving love, but instead, I criticized her for having the same lack of emotional expression as I did. In my head, women expressed their emotions, and I felt cheated that I was with someone who couldn't. It's funny how sometimes the women men end up with are either the exact mirror reflection of us or the exact opposite. It wasn't until I took a break from relationships and actually had time to analyze my behavioral patterns to see where my lack of emotional expression really was stemming from.

THE ROOTS OF IT

I didn't grow up in a household where love was easily, openly or frequently expressed. The greatest form of love that I saw and learned from my upbringing was a sense of obligation. Obligation as in "this is what married people do" or "this is what a mother or a father does." I never saw passionate, expressive, emotional love in my father's marriage. It wasn't something that I ever learned how to express or use and I always noticed that there was a shortage of it in my house because so many other families I knew were so much more affectionate with each other. I'm now certain that this upbringing of mine has something to do with why I always sought out a partner who would be openly expressive in her emotional love for me. Every relationship I found myself in where the woman lacked affection for me, I'd run away from her. I'd end relationships for other things much more trivial than that, but without affection, I was certain to make a fast exit. I know myself well enough now to pinpoint this and be real about how I can improve while also knowing that this is something that I do look for when courting a woman.

If something in your upbringing is the reason you have a guard up and won't let a woman into your heart, you must first come face to face with that truth. A lot of us men find all kinds of reasons why we don't express our love and why we won't let a woman in, blaming it on something the woman does or doesn't do when the root problem is all within us. Yes, she makes mistakes, much like you, but mistakes don't warrant bad treatment or a lack of love. Man, I'm telling you, this is embedded in your subconscious and can haunt you for the rest of your life if you don't deal with it on your own first. This is the type of stuff that affects how children perceive love and how they eventually search for love. This kind of emotional shutdown is also one of the reasons why some men get cheated on by women who love them. She never felt like she was getting enough love from the man she loved, and when what seemed like an opportunity to receive love came along, she took it! Can you blame her? Yes! You can, but if she's accustomed to running into a brick wall when addressing her need for love from a man, then I can honestly say that I know many men who would do the same thing. It won't matter for long how good a provider you are or how good of a father you are if you can't express love to the woman you say you love. Most women are fueled by expressions of love, and if you find yourself to be the kind of man who doesn't give that, then a woman who is needy for love will likely grow unsatisfied.

Too many women have been dragged through the mud by "good" men who refused to fix problems within themselves that they know they need to fix. Many men are easily the good guy but choose to play the villain in their own movie. A lot of men don't want to face the pain of why they've become like this, but you must if you want happiness for yourself and your family. There are so many different issues that we face through the ills of society, and many of us are running from them or worse—we take those problems and hide them from the women we are with. Having been taught to be strong, many men assumed that a measurement of strength was our ability to keep problems that we face to ourselves. The superficial shell of manhood that this has created still sets the standard of how men behave and are perceived today. We're macho men who have been hurt and don't know how to give or receive love.

WE'RE ALL WOUNDED

The world has scarred you as a man, but she's been scarred by the world, too. She's among the walking wounded just like you, and sometimes the least you can do is create an outlet for expression of these hurts you both carry. Be a leader and do that for yourself; she deserves to know why you behave the way you do. Many men expect women to provide them with a shoulder to lean on but opt not to lean on their shoulders by refusing to express themselves. It seems like simple common sense to say you're hungry when you're hungry, but why is not common sense to say I love you when you feel it? Some dangle emotional expression as a game they play to keep the women in their life yearning for more. With everything I talk about in the other chapters of this book, it should be made clear that if you have to play with her emotions to keep her engaged with you, then she's not the one for you. We have to outgrow girls who get bored easily and move on when they're not getting all of our attention; she's an eternal 16-year-old who wants nothing more than to be admired, and she keeps the pressure on you to admire her or she'll find someone else who will. You shouldn't have to create or play emotional mind games to keep her around.

It's not a crime to express how you feel. And by that, I don't mean yelling and screaming when you're upset, but smiling and laughing when you're happy, complimenting when you genuinely like something and saying how you feel when you feel it rather than waiting until it's built up and comes spewing out in rage. You have to be able to look at how you express yourself and figure out where you got that from. As much as everyone wants to say that they're unique, we've all been influenced by others in ways that we aren't totally aware of. When that happens, there becomes a blurry line between who you are and who you've been influenced to be, but many men won't do the self-work to find out their true voice and their true image. A man's true voice is transformational when he begins to listen to it. When you can hear yourself clearly, you can execute your vision; you can speak your heart's desires and those desires require emotional intelligence to be expressed efficiently.

Major influences that cause men to close up include, but are not limited to:

1. **Media influence**—Men have been influenced to be tough & strong rather than kind and practical. Many of us wanted to be gangsters, playboys, and athletes based on the influence of movies and TV. Depending on where you may come from, the influence to be strong and dominant might be more or less. The world identifies strength as a defining characteristic of a man based on imagery and influence. When we seek to prove this to the world, the ego soon takes over and shuts down our emotional intelligence. This isn't manhood, and it's sad to see how much damage this has caused.

2. **Mommy issues**—Mom's the first person you want to please in life. She's all of our first love. But many boys struggle when their mothers struggle, and if Mom had it really rough, it has a way of affecting us for a lifetime. Everyone loves their mom, but sometimes mom wasn't ready to be a mom when she became one. Boys coming from the inner cities and single mom homes not only had to bear the burden of not having a father, but also the burden of a world that mistreated and overworked their mothers. It can be hard to recover from never seeing your mother happy. If this is an issue of yours, you must address it because self-love is the beginning of happiness.

3. **Abandonment**—Some boys never had parents at all. If you had one or both parents and still have issues, imagine what life was like for he who had none. The pain of Mom leaving and never returning or not ever knowing who your father was is some deep stuff that affects many men to their core well into their adult lives.

4. **Abuse**—I've had friends who've suffered abuse from frustrated, overworked, alcoholic and drug addicted parents. Take parents out of the equation and you have bullies in all forms who prey on boys; sexual predators, rapists, thugs, drug dealers, the military, rebel warriors, systematic racism, political schemes and more. Abuse doesn't always have to be physical because much of the abuse we experience is psychological torment designed to influence your behavior and your output. Many boys are targeted with

self-defeating concepts about themselves that stunt their growth and pools them into societal categories. This is a systematic form of abuse that is widespread.

5. **Environment**—Let's not pretend that many of us didn't have to come out of some of the toughest parts of town or the toughest homes to make it to where we are today. Some neighborhoods don't let you out, especially if you already are facing socio-economic struggles and parental issues or lack thereof. Many of our environments have been engineered against us. Many boys don't mature into men because they drown from the pressures of their environments—that environment could be their neighborhood, school, family, peers, etc. The ones who make it out don't make it out without a few scars and bruises that they still deal with in their manhood. For many the abuse endures as men.

Many of these things limit the capacity for sound development and create conflict in the mind, which creates conflict in relationships and casts a cloud of confusion over the families and children a man has. However, not everyone recognizes these problems and figure it into their rehabilitation process. It's important to have the protection you need to grow and develop to your full potential, but even with adequate protection, many of our boys have been subject to one or a few of the above problematic situations.

Man to Man: So what happens when you're in touch with your emotions and your intuition?

You grow! You develop more evenly because you need strength and compassion together at the same time to remain balanced. Life is about balance, and the imbalanced man is highly combustible. If he's too strong, he'll harden and eventually crack from inside or outside pressure. If he's too soft, he'll be penetrated by the force, manipulations and influences of others. The current times we live in alter much of who we are as men to align us with the national agenda of gaining power and conquering others. Unfortunately, it's not just men who exhibit the lack of compassion. Women suffer increasingly from the lack of a true heart centered connection because they have had to become so tough in a world that is gunning for us all.

We have to be willing to reset ourselves. Many of us don't know where to start, but it's easier than you think. Look at your life. Look at all the hardship you or your loved ones have had to endure. Feel that pain! Feel how wrong it was and refuse to accept it as "the way things are." We are what we think, and most people try not to think about the pain they've experienced because it hurts so bad, but ignoring it leaves more room for the problem to thrive. If you're not the victim, having compassion for the victims helps to bring presence of mind to the source of the problem. Compassion isn't just about a few words of condolences you express to others. Compassion is fuel for change. If more men embrace the atrocities that have happened to them and the women they love instead of pretending it didn't happen, then more men with this presence of mind can collectively bring forth a compassionate change in our world. It's like group meditation. We must all come together and shine our light in the dark places, even the corners no one pays attention to and place a collective healing energy on it to eradicate it from the face of this planet. We have that power only when we choose to embrace the pain. For too long, we've been trying to hide our vulnerability from the world, but there's power in it. The more men who consciously decide that they will be a tool used to fight hate, violence, egocentrism, the more successes we'll have for mankind as a whole. It's something men must do collectively. And I believe men can take this lead to restore peace, love, and unity to the masses when we let go of the ego's need for power and allow compassion to be our form of politics.

THE IMPORTANCE OF VULNERABILITY

I must admit that I've made a lot of excuses over the years for not opening up to women. There was a time that I wasn't quite sure how to open up. If an attempt to be vulnerable with a woman was met with the wrong response, I usually took that as a sign that she wasn't the one for me. Most men, myself included, are looking for a woman who is more in touch with her emotions than we are. I was always careful not to put too much of my precious little feelings out there to a potentially unresponsive woman. Male vulnerability is such a fragile thing, and most of us just don't want to have to dish out our feelings too often. I know I don't. But I'm learning there's value in sharing your vulnerability; not only to the woman you love but with the world.

It's one thing to open up and spill your guts about how you feel about her, why you love her and why you need her, but there's so much more to a man opening up and actually being vulnerable. In our minds, it's like we're honoring her by sharing things with her that we wouldn't normally share. Where we get it wrong is when we expect one particular response and feel rejected when we don't get it. It doesn't mean she doesn't care. She may not know how to relate to you because she's not used to men expressing themselves. I've been down that road where I've shared things about my past that literally drew a blank stare from a woman. That's so uncomfortable. But you may have to swallow your pride and accept that she doesn't understand your struggle, and she might not be the one for you. If she doesn't get you, just view it as practice. Don't shut the door on yourself. Sometimes when your emotional needs fall on deaf ears, it's a lesson for you to learn that expression is expression; it doesn't always need a response. Get it out and get used to getting it out. The right woman will respond to you based on your needs.

SEXUAL EMOTIONS

Many guys get super emotional and openly expressive only with the woman they sleep with. I'm not saying anything's wrong with that. I'm just hoping that if you've done that before, but the relationship didn't work out, that you remain open to expressing yourself more freely rather than only as a byproduct of a sexual relationship. Vulnerability doesn't make you soft, but sex shouldn't be the trigger for your vulnerability.

In fact, learning how to share pieces of your vulnerability early on can teach you a lot about the woman you're pursuing. When you share your vulnerability with her, the response you get from her can help you decide if you feel comfortable sharing more personal matters with her. For a man to develop a strong bond with a woman, he must feel like he can tell her anything. She has to feel like a safe place he can always go to without backlash. You can't only tell her you love her and you need her when you're making love to her and no other time.

I had to analyze my past relationships to see if I was the kind of guy who only caught feelings or got emotional with them when we were intimate. I'm not saying anything is wrong with that, but understand what's going on with you if this is your pattern. This can be a set up for disaster if the emotional connection is based entirely on this sexual connection. We don't all understand the mystical connections that sex creates between a man and woman, but many of us have felt it. It's a good thing to want to share more emotional intimacy with the person you're sharing physical intimacy with. But sexual expression with the wrong person can lead to some really bad situations. It's not automatic that because you two are having a good sexual relationship that she's the one; it doesn't mean she cares or is even in love with you, either. If things don't work out—because of you or her—she doesn't owe you anything because you shared your heart with her. She doesn't have to stay with you, and she's free to move on as she pleases. Good sex has its effects, but don't allow it to make you feel things for someone who you would otherwise have no true connection with.

I know many men who've closed up because they feel their vulnerability was betrayed. You shared with her some things you wouldn't normally tell anyone, but you guys break up, and she spills all the beans and even uses it against you because she was hurt or wanted to be vindictive. I've had that happen to me, where a bitter ex hacked into my database to contact women from my past to tell them negative things about me. Not many women who truly love you are willing to throw themselves under the bus in an attempt to cause you pain.

Our relationship was over, and there was no coming back to her like I did in the past and she knew it this time. I felt that perhaps she would address her side of why I chose to break things off, but instead, she chose not to address any role she played. I felt utterly violated by everything that transpired and there weren't any conversations to be had about what she did or why she did it or even how I felt about it. She ultimately made a fool out of herself in an attempt to slam me and proved to be someone who had little integrity. She always had the option to be humble about it or create more problems to hide the truth, but ultimately we both know the truth. I knew that I was taking a risk by sharing my vulnerability with her when I did it, but sometimes you have to take risks to free yourself. I feel a lot more comfortable about sharing myself with my future partner because of this experience, but I learned from it. I know better than to allow sex to be the reason I feel comfortable enough to share heartfelt emotions with a woman. The connection has to be deeper than sex.

Her spilling certain beans didn't bother me as much as the response I initially got when I did decide to open up to her. She was stone cold; she didn't care about my growth and development as a man. She knew her place was only secure within my dysfunction, so me opening up to identify problems that needed to be fixed would surely open wounds she wasn't ready for anyone to touch. I knew then that perhaps her issues were haunting her too much for her to empathize with me and I wasn't upset about it. It really doesn't matter what you share in your intimate space with a woman, just know that if she ends up using it against you in any shape or form, it shouldn't be the reason you can no longer trust women. The lesson is taking more time to get to know her before sex. I know how hard it can be to trust and be vulnerable, but if you want better, you must be willing to share your heart outside of the bedroom, too.

EXPRESSION IS THE KEY

Emotions don't have to be all about sensitivity and romance. It could be as simple as expressing your deepest fears or sharing an experience that you rarely ever discuss. There are many different ways to express your emotions and show levels of your vulnerability. I consider it to be an important thing for a growing and evolving man to do. If you've learned the value of being careful and selective about the women you choose, then showing your softer side will eventually become easier for you to do. You just don't want to be the guy who has all his emotions and vulnerability bottled up; living like that will make you a ticking time bomb.

Your ideal woman will respect your expressed emotions and have a place in her heart for your vulnerability. If she feels honored to be courting you, then she will value that you want to share it with her and will look at it as a sign that you want to grow closer to her. Because it is. Most men and women carry some kind of baggage into relationships, but we must be willing to help the other person unpack their bags without expecting anything in return. Moments when you take the time to express things to a woman are some of the most ideal for growth in a relationship. Expressing emotions and vulnerability don't mean the same thing to every woman, so the key here is going through the process of selecting the right partner who you understand how to communicate with.

SEX AIN'T BETTER THAN LOVE

In my last pseudo-relationship, where she literally made jokes about packing up my dick and taking it everywhere with her, I would tell her that while I've "been around," not many women can say that they had my heart. She just didn't get it at all. She thought that she'd just put it on me, and I'd go get her a ring and worship the ground she walked on. I used to tell her crazy ass all the time that good sex doesn't mean you know someone or even love them. Loving someone takes a lot more than opening your legs, so sex has never convinced me that any woman loved me nor has it been my reason for loving a woman. The aftereffect of good sex has confused me before, but it's never given me any feeling of assurance that I could bank on. This one was the type who came from a past where love and sex were like the same thing to her. She had some serious trust issues stemming from her parents' marriage. She didn't want to be the conventional loyal wife her mother was, and her rebellion landed her in bed with many men. I later learned that sex was what she loved, not the men. Men need to learn to recognize when a woman is hot in the pants and has more mileage on her vagina than her actual heart. She had sexual experiences with men, not experience actually loving men. I always knew the difference because my heart and my penis live in totally different places. And while the desires of my penis might drive me to some wild and crazy extents, I never mistook any of my sexual adventures for love. Great sex usually equals crazy, not love.

As detached as many men may be, many of us do have keys to our hearts. Some of us just have to find those keys and cut copies for the people we love. Sex and love aren't the same, but to an inexperienced young person, it might feel like the same thing. We all have given out the keys to our heart based on heightened physical and emotional feelings. I know I get all dreamy when the loving is good. I've always been the type that's more expressive when the sex is good, but I've had to change that to make certain that hearts and minds can align before hormones dominate the playing field. The older you get, the more dependent you are on the love you receive from your significant other. Nobody wants to have to pack their bags and move on to someone entirely new every 15 minutes in love.

In those relationships that are heavily dependent on sex, just take away sex and see how well you two sync. Women do this all the time to men and replace sex with a line of interrogation about how he feels about her. Why can't you do the same thing to evaluate the actual substance you have in your relationship? Something is wrong if you can only see eye to eye when there's consistent sex. I've been on both sides of this equation: once where I wasn't getting any, and I literally sunk the relationship. There was also a time I wasn't giving any, and she sunk the relationship.

But boy how some things always come full circle. She's a potential enemy of yours if she's not interested in the substance you bring other than sex. And I know many men don't often experience women like these, but my evaluation of past relationships and flings has led me to two-three women who were strictly interested in getting their rocks off. So much so that they'd risk a lot for it, just like a man. The high a man gets from that is unprecedented, but the lows that come with someone whose primary love for you is based on sex are pretty low. They can and will hurt you because physical expression is their only expression and when they feel like the "love" you give to them is being taken away, they will sometimes resort to attempting to physically harm you. The intent is to control your love by force.

Rising from the lows of sex is an act of self-love that will challenge you mentally, physically, and emotionally. For many men, it is just easier to tell her you love her during sex whether you love her or not. For some women, that is the only form of love they've ever received from a man. People coming from these roots have had to struggle to love themselves and have grown accustomed to accepting whatever form of love they attract when in this stage of disorientation. You'll find that many of these people love very conditionally because they've never been loved unconditionally by anyone other than maybe their parents. They do for someone with the intent of receiving. They love you with full expectation that you must love them back—despite what you're going through in your life, and despite what they've put you through. If what you're going through keeps you from loving them, then they're prepared for some kind of war to get what they want or to separate from you. Sex to them is the barometer of how well the relationship is performing and if there's no sex, then in their mind the love is headed right out the front door. You must be cautious that you are not this person because it's quite common for men to be detached and go through the motions with women for the sake of busting a nut, then calling it love. We've got to open our hearts and empathize with each other. Sexual love is fantastic if it stems from true love of self and unconditional love for another.

MOVING ON WHEN THERE
ARE CHILDREN INVOLVED

WHEN YOU'VE TRULY MOVED ON from her, you're not going to have sex with her ever again nor entertain the idea of a relationship with her anymore. And it's even harder to move on when there are children involved. The mother(s) of your children could either be easy prey for you when you want sex and comfort or a predator who knows how to work your weaknesses to get you into bed. Both scenarios will boil down to the strength of your willpower.

People find it difficult to move on from past relationships because they never stop sleeping with each other long enough to detach. It's not just women who get attached, either. Men tend to be just as attached as women are, especially if it's really good sex. Men just don't like to admit it. I know men who've literally been turned out by women who fucked them unlike they've ever been fucked before. When children are involved, there's so much more emotional connection that comes with the sex that incentivizes men to continue the sexual relationship even if they don't want a future with the mom. Men get caught up like this without even knowing it. The point here, though, is that eventually you snap out of being caught up, and then you must close the door on the mother(s) of your children if she's not the one for you. It's only so long you can stay in these dead end situations, even if she is the mother of your child.

ANALYZE THE DEMISE

You have to be able to analyze why things didn't work out with you and the mother(s) of your children as you move onto greener pastures. For me, I'll always bite the bullet and say that it was I who didn't want to be with them. I'll be honest and say that it took me too long to close the door than I should have. There was never a point where I was consistently happy enough with myself or them, but I take responsibility for that these days. They'll never hear me say anything about what they did or didn't do. Ultimately, I'm the common denominator. It was I who didn't understand how I failed myself by not going with my gut instincts and intuition. Had I taken a strong position on what I wanted for myself, I would've saved myself a lot of time and energy. I have to be honest with myself and admit that during that stage of my life I was more interested in sex than relationships and had this skewed perspective that I could just move on when I felt like it. My cut off game was once a work of art, but I had lost it. I got soft, got reckless and women got pregnant.

Given my circumstances, I was immature about love and surprisingly also immature about sex. When a woman chooses to have sex with you, whether she admits it or not, subconsciously she wants more than just sex, either from you or in general. Good women are choosers and usually have plenty of options to choose from outside of just you. But there is a sizeable portion of women who are just as oversexed as men are and who are more than willing to sleep with you based on physical assets alone. It's not often that you find the one here, but it can happen.

When it hasn't worked out with the mom, and you have to move on, you must move on with all your goals and priorities first in line. When you do the things that allow you to create for yourself and your family, it becomes less stressful to deal with the mom because you bring a lot to the table for the child, and your stability also benefits her and gives her a sense of security. Women won't always admit this, but it's true. If a woman is physically attractive, loving and is a help to you and your family, why would a man leave? Well, realistically some men must admit that they were sleeping with someone they had no business sleeping with, and then tried to rush a relationship that they would never otherwise want, and it eventually failed. It's easy to point fingers in situations like these, but the wise thing is knowing who you're with and if they add to you or subtract from you. If she doesn't add to you, then she subtracts from you, and it's OK to peacefully part ways from these kinds of women.

VALUABLE LESSONS

This chapter is heavily based on many of the lessons I learned while trying to make it work out "for the child." I'm glad that I was able to release myself from this form of bondage. I had to learn not to need to control the situation and begin to work on me enough to make improvements for my own welfare. This is America, and almost anywhere in the world you go to, if a woman is sure that you're the one for her, then she will likely have no problem conceiving a child for you. You don't have to stick around, but those who stick around usually do so because they really like the woman and can see a future with her. That's pretty much the special sauce that makes even an unprepared man try to work things out rather than moving on. Today, the women that are propped up in front of everyone are women who aren't wives but are independent-minded women with very little capacity for family building. I'm not saying they can't be wives—the vast majority just aren't. In today's world, we have a plethora of women who are perceived as valuable based almost entirely on their appearance. Typically, if these women marry, they do so to have babies and then divorce for financial purposes; they aren't necessarily women who want to be relegated to all of the role that comes with the title of being a wife. Very similarly, we have many varieties of the men who don't stick around to father children and are uninterested in being husbands. The rationale here is that it's not worth the headache to work things out with someone who you'll never see eye to eye with. Judge this man if you wish, but he's likely to be happier than the guy who stuck around only to be tormented by a woman who he would not have any relations with if it were not for a child. This is a hard position for a man who doesn't know himself to be in. It can confuse a man and lead to depression.

If you're in this predicament, there will come a time when you realize that being dragged back and forth between women and children is a dead end scenario for your ability to prosper in life. It only adds stress and a higher potential for drama to your plate. Whether you're trying to make it work for the children or you're trying to peacefully co-parent with someone who is consistently difficult, these "situation-ships" always fail for two major reasons: 1) men don't stick around for women who they no longer like or love and 2) having children, but no wife isn't a real family unit. When a man decides that he wants a family rather than just children, and he puts his hands to the work of manifesting that, then that family he builds with his wife will take first priority. If you have a child in another house, you'd have to leave your children in your house if the other child needs you. Some single mothers feel that if they had a child with you before you finally settle down with someone new, then she and that child come first in your life. She's wrong! You come first. That's the only way you'll be able to prosper well enough to support your children. Men with children before their marriage must seek to have all their children under one roof because stretching between two or more is a drain on their resources and leaves that outside child out of their immediate protection. When you move on, you must think wife. She must accept and love you first and be willing to play a motherly role to your pre-marriage children as well. The family you build with your wife comes first.

PEACE OFFERINGS

What's important to understand when you move on from the mother, is that there will be no peace moving forward if there are no agreements that can serve as the foundation of your new relationship.

New boundaries must be set to where it is clear that the intimate relationship aspect is over. And don't fool yourself about being able to all of a sudden get along with her when you've never gotten along before. I say humility and accountability should be any man's saving grace for moving forward peacefully in situations like these, but being humble doesn't mean you'll be forgiven or that she won't still play wicked games. The truth about being in this space with a woman is that for many women there's this Texas-sized sense of entitlement they feel when they have a child for you. And trust me, a woman who feels this way likely feels as if you owe her for that child she birthed. Add that to the heartbreak of knowing that you two will never be together again, and that's enough for a woman who has had your child to hate your guts for a long time. I really do understand it more now that I've seen emotional fallouts happen right in front of my face. I do hold myself accountable for the role I played in disappointing them, but when it's all said and done, I wouldn't have been happy "doing it for the kids" so I had to move on. In my situations, I allowed women to play star roles in my life, and it did nothing but cost me valuable time and energy. I'll never do that again. She can't play any role in my life if she's intent on being problematic. You must communicate and behave in a peaceful manner in order to demand it in return. Even if she is a troublemaker, remove your ego and never allow yourself to be offended or to get defensive.

Be the first to move on peacefully—forgiving all that happened between you two. If you can't be the first, be the second. Just don't be the guy who is still caught up with what his child's mother does or says. Do what you have to do on your end to show that you're about moving forward peacefully even if your actions ended the relationship. If you have children together, and you intend on being involved in your children's lives without having to jump through fire rings, you must come in peace, and you must be humble despite the response. What you don't allow is for her to continually cause you losses just because she can.

DISAGREEMENTS & SOLUTIONS

There will always be standards that even two people who can't see eye to eye can share in common. Find them, highlight them and work on agreeing with them for the sake of the children involved. If you can't agree to basic standards of how you want your children raised, then you must file court ordered documentation to allow more of your input in how the child is raised. If she is determined to raise your son to be a Christian, but you're a Muslim, then she's willing to undermine you to get her way. Do not allow this. Make her put some respect on your name, especially if you're an equally contributing father. Most men won't take the position I choose to take when it comes to certain things pertaining to children from failed relationships because they feel social pressure to stick around and be passive about whatever she wants to do with their child. Unfortunately, not enough men know what they want for their children and thereby end up not speaking up for how they want their children raised. If a woman feels a child is the father's responsibility to take care of, then she should leave that in his hands when the child is old enough. She can do the nurturing and all the other maternal things, but if she squarely expects you to do the bulk of the heavy lifting when it comes to supporting and raising the child, then she needs to get out of your way so you can do that. When she can't do that, it's just another sign of the fact that you and this person are not in agreement. In situations like these, if you can't get the legal support you need, you must still stand firmly on your position. I've seen too many of my peers and colleagues who never got the chance to spend adequate time with their own fathers because their mothers wanted to have sole authority over their lives, even if it meant excluding the father. You might think you two can come to a solution, but don't kid yourself if the history shows that you can't. What you need is money for a lawyer, other than that, stay very far away from her. She's on a vendetta to hurt you. She thinks that it's OK to keep up second-class behavior while the child is young, but as the child grows so does her erratic behavior. She can't control her emotions, and if you slip up and end up sleeping with her at any point, then you're almost giving her permission to be an asshole to you. You won't get a fair shot at reasonable solutions until you both have detached from each other and even then, it may not mean she's over you or over the pain she associates with you.

DON'T PRETEND AT ALL

What you can't do is pretend you like someone who is committed to making your life difficult. When you're ready to move on, and she isn't, you must expect that she's going to have vengeance in her heart. You can't ignore her hurt feelings, but by no means should you shy away from pointing out what's obvious—she's using the child as a means to inflict emotional pain on you because she has no other power card to play. Call it what it is, but remain calm when you speak the truth. The truth doesn't need to be shouted or argued for it to be the truth. If the truth hurts, then prepare to deal with someone who will try to inflict pain instead of being truthful. Make sure you're not the one in denial and not accepting the truth of the circumstances you're in. When you realize who you're dealing with, you can stand on your position and not become angered or emotional in the sight of her challenging you. When you can do this, you are now facing your truth without fighting for it. You don't have to behave erratically to show her you don't approve or agree, and you don't have to be mean or denigrate her in any way in response to her behavior.

In my book of baby mama drama, I say don't put up with any of the post-relationship drama that she will throw to keep you tied to her. This is why you need time to yourself where you can get to actually leave things behind for good. I had a bad separation with the mother of my child when she got upset that I wasn't ready to have my other child sleep in the same bed as us. Even though it never happened before, she was determined that it was time for it to happen, and when I said no, she went to bed angry and woke up in the morning ready to fight. I begged her not to do this in front of the children and when she chose to literally have an emotional breakdown, I had no choice

33

but to leave. I grabbed some of my stuff, went down to my car and on my way back up to her apartment I saw my three-year-old outside of the door looking around in bewilderment. I knocked on the door and when she opened it, I asked her why was my child locked outside the door instead of on the couch watching TV, and she tried to fight me. That was all I needed to assure me that I was done with her for good. But realistically, it had been done long before that. My three-year-old would then tell her mother all about it and it became evident that it was a traumatic experience for her because of how much she spoke about it. I've never felt safe in that woman's presence ever since. After about a week of separating myself from her, she found every conceivable way to reach me and slander me—through my immediate family members, through social media, etc. She'd call my mother, father and brother to tell them things to hurt my character. She'd even contact an ex from over two years prior to slander my name because she felt she still liked me. She hacked into my social media profiles to cause strife. She created a hashtag for me called #veganpenis and posted about me being good for nothing but sex. She revealed that she had terminated a previous pregnancy and that I would theoretically have more children if it weren't for that- to my Instagram followers. She did all this in public in attempt to side rail me because I ended the relationship when she felt she should have. I never complained to her or got upset in her presence, not once. I never made mention to her of anything she did. I just took some screenshots of everything and carried on because I was certain of two things 1) I couldn't care less about her existence outside of being the mother of my child and 2) there'd be no sequel to us.

FOCUSING ON YOU & YOUR RELATIONSHIP WITH YOUR CHILDREN

When it's time to go in separate directions, the biggest issues that surface will be about money and happiness. She's going to need money from you, but she's also looking for someone new who's going to finally "make her happy" and take care of her in ways you never did. She wants to be able to show you she can replace you with another man who will buy into her damsel in distress story enough to want to give her everything she never got from you. You should wish her all the best from the bottom of your heart. As long as her search for someone new doesn't hinder your role in your children's lives, she can look for love all she wants. A mature man desires a good, strong relationship with his children that's reinforced by his presence and the direction he provides in their life. When they are under four years old, it's fair to say that they're still mostly mommy's baby. What matters is how accessible you are to them and how well you develop your relationship with them so they will honor and respect you as they grow. If you're in a situation where the mother discredits you, it may be an uphill battle, but understand that parental relationships go through different stages in every decade. If the mother is committed to causing disruptions to your peace, you must distance yourself from her sphere of influence. You must have control over an environment where the standards are according to your lifestyle and your children see you for who you are, rather than what their opposing mother wants them to believe.

Never play the game with her where you're trying to prove yourself to her to remain in your children's lives. You have to believe that bonding with your children doesn't always happen when they're young and tender and can happen at any age in their life. It can happen in their pre-teen or teenage years and it can also happen in their twenties and beyond. If you're a high value man then you're a high value parent who can continue to add value to your children's life experiences even in their older years. Early difficulties with mothers drive away some fathers permanently, but you must remain open to being there for them when they need you and be able to communicate that to them. I'm in my early 30s now and my relationship with both my parents is constantly evolving. These days my father is so much more understanding and encouraging, whereas in my younger age, I felt he couldn't relate to me. You never know when you'll hit your stride with your children, so remain open, but most importantly stay dedicated to living the best life for you that benefits them. If you have a great life that you live, you can always share that with them- at any age.

I mismanaged my relationships with both women who had children for me. They should've been long released from my bondage to go their own separate ways, but I held on because I was fearful of how a major separation would affect the children. In one case it was problematic from the very beginning because having a child wasn't truly what she wanted. I wasn't what she dreamed of and our differences where huge in the beginning and still are now that years have gone by. I was naïve to think that we'd all just focus on what's best for the children after I had created a situation where I added to the pain these women were already experiencing in their lives. This is where sometimes it can be difficult to actually focus on the children in the aftermath of messy breakups. In most cases both men and women are still deeply entrenched in their feelings and tend to behave erratically to show just how unhappy they are. As a man we must hold ourselves accountable for our decisions and sometimes even for her behavioral responses to us. And we must be willing to be patient while accepting that this person may become very difficult to deal with when hurt; so much so that you may have to separate from their presence. However, you must be willing to forgive and move forward- no matter how badly she attempts to hurt you. It can be a slow process.

When you've wronged someone you must embody humility. But as a humble lion, not a humble little bitch who will put up with any kind of drama to see and spend time with your children. A woman can do that on her own time, not on my time. You must be able to put on your big boy pants and step up to the plate to clear past relational issues that have become problematic in your relationship with her. For some women it takes years to move on, but often times it takes this long because men are still dibbling and dabbling with their children's mothers when they shouldn't be. That's giving her permission to misbehave, especially if you go back and forth to each other without any real intention of staying together. Moving on means you refuse to entertain anymore foolishness from her, but it also means you're not being inappropriate with her in any way. Leaving her alone like this might be her worst nighmare, but your dedication to it may be able to bring peace to your relationship. When you move on with dignity and respect, yet experience difficulties from her anyway, you must be willing to defend that position because you two are no longer romantically involved. The focus should be on the child and you must make sure of it by dealing with her with integrity and never allowing yourself to get sidetracked by her haymakers which often include reminding you of how you used to be or what you did years ago. I understand that moving on is a process that takes some women a long time to go through, but I'm not the one to be dragging behind her if she's not ready to let go of me. No man should allow this. I suggest you cut her loose whether she likes it or not. If she's not the one, let her go.

FOCUS ON YOUR IDEAL FAMILY

Moving on meant that I had to remember that the ideal family environment that I wanted for myself was definitely not going to happen with my previous situation. I don't believe in settling for a life you don't want. Everyone likes to say that a woman will move on, but if you look around at the way things are, a lot of women don't move on successfully. In some cases, they don't want to move on because you're the one they still want—despite the disappointment and hurt. I've decided to free myself from any idea of settling down with any woman that I feel is not right for me. I've made a promise to myself that I will only go after who I feel I have the best chance of living my dream life with. I want a family and I won't settle for being dragged between homes by women who don't have my best interest at heart.

If I can't learn to love her soon enough, then my motto is to move on fast. Most women want to be loved intensely and passionately, and that's easy to do when that's the woman who you truly want to be with. But if the love isn't there, pretending is a prison you don't want to end up stuck in. You don't even want to do that for children- trust me. Get the family life you want!

THE MOTHER ISN'T INCLUDED IF SHE'S RESISTANT

When you're realistically moving on, the issue that becomes most important is that you establish a standard for yourself as a father, given the new circumstances. The circumstance is that you're not with the mother of the child at all (and she hates your guts). Because of that she's ran off in her pursuit of happiness, and now you see your child less. Or she lives 15 minutes away, but plays keep away with the child. An important component to moving on from failed relationships that involve children is knowing what's truly best for the children. Don't automatically assume that because she's the woman, the child is better off with her. Be conscientious about a lot of different factors involved in the bigger picture such as the age of the child, the child's emotional needs, who can provide the child with more of what the child needs, the environment, finances, etc. Single women with children don't move on to greener pastures so easily. Don't believe the sitcoms you see on TV. Many of those frogs that she now wants to kiss in her quest to find a prince will be exposed to your children and you must have a realistic gauge to measure that impact on your child.

What you can't do is lose your lid because you want to control the entire situation. You'll end up losing a lot more sleep by behaving like this. And if she knows how to push your buttons, you may also be at risk of losing your freedom because she'll push these buttons of yours and call the police on you. As hard as it may be to move on, do it from a firm position and remain in control of your emotions. All you ever have to do is live the life you know you came here to live. This is why space is necessary and this is why seeking your purpose is so important to your overall happiness. After you've healed and moved on, if you choose someone new to build your ideal family unit with, then most of your focus should be there where your presence has the largest impact. When you can turn your focus to this, you'll become determined to build a family unit that will include your children who don't live with you. It's not an easy process to endure, but its part of being a man who can recover from his mistakes and shortcomings. Don't stay stuck on women because of children. Make up your mind what role you want to play and execute that role with precision. Don't' try to control a woman you can't control, so save yourself the drama. Learn to be positive about your chosen lifestyle, and be 100% assured that it will be a benefit to your children.

A NEW WOMAN

I don't recommend men to take a break from relationships for them to keep repeating the same mistakes with women. I challenge you to make noticeable improvements while on a break so that way you can better qualify or eliminate women you are interested in. When you have children, there are two perspectives that you need to overcome with your new partner:

1) How women view you as a "baby daddy"

If you meet a woman who has no children and you have two, please believe that her family is likely to be totally against her being with you. Some men and women are raised to avoid being stepparents. I know I was taught that to a certain extent, but I still dated women with children even when I had no children of my own. But can you blame concerned parents and family members?

In my case, I have two children with two different women! Some mothers and fathers would launch a full-blown protest to keep me away from their daughters. I understand their concern and if a woman you're interested in is very close to family who disapprove of you, that relationship can become a battleground with her family having home field advantage. I could care less about situations like these because it's their concern, not mine. In my case, it's clear to the world that I failed miserably at two relationships that involved children so they should question your ability to succeed in a new relationship where a third child could potentially be added to the mix. If anyone in her family is man or woman enough to address this respectably, then it's a great opportunity to talk about your experiences and the work you do now that will guide you to success. Hold yourself accountable for your past, but you don't have to kiss up too much.

When a mature woman has chosen you, it's your job to make sure she has a full understanding of how her life will be impacted because of you and your children. If she's informed then you should trust her on her decision. If she's strong, she'll stick by her decision and stick to the plan you two have created. If she's weak, you'll see her wavering because of the influence of others and it'll become easy to make a decision to move on without her.

2) Expectations of her as a potential "stepmom"

It can be a very delicate situation when it comes to getting comfortable with the role your new partner will play with your children, but it's not as important as the role you already play in your children's lives. You have to be able to hold your own as a father first. You don't have to be the perfect father, you just have to be doing the work that it requires because a woman you're seriously involved with can be an extension of you in many ways. And if you're a single dad who can use the help when you're alone with your children, then it could be a great thing for you. Ideally, the person you're with shares many of the same lifestyle principles as you, but it doesn't mean you guys will react to every dilemma pertaining to children in the same way. Some women without children have as many maternal instincts as women with children while others may be clueless on what to do in some situations. It won't take much time in the presence of your children for you to figure things out. If she's a keeper, she'll definitely find ways to be a big help with the kids, but you must give her time to adjust to this role before you're totally committed to her being the woman in your life.

The goal is not to overload her with what is your responsibility. Especially not in the beginning before she's spent some quality time with you and your children together. Some women will know exactly what to do and when to do it when it comes to children, but some will struggle to learn the ropes. Be patient and wise because there are many factors that affect this situation, like how much time your children spend with you, how good she is with children, how much you trust her ability to supervise your children and the nature of the relationship with you and the children's mother(s). The goal is for there to be no pressure on her to be a step-mom.

JUST MOVE ON

There are several types of moving on situations, but none quite as complicated as those situations involving children. Once it's been determined that the mother of your child/children isn't the one you want to be with, you must prepare mentally, emotionally and financially for everything that comes with moving on- like child support and petty games with the children. A man must be firm on his decision to move on when he's made that decision and shouldn't allow any form of manipulations that she may try to keep you from moving on.

Whatever it is, just move on and keep moving even if she isn't over you. Keep moving when you feel down, and you want to call her for comfort. Keep moving when she keeps the child away from you and you miss them. Keep moving when she tells you she wants you guys to be a family. Just keep moving because the most telling sign of any relationship is why you're not together, not why you should get back together.

TAKING A BREAK FROM RELATIONSHIPS

IF YOU'RE A MAN WHO has dated a slew of women, has had more one-night stands than successful relationships, have had a few stalkers, a couple victims, more than one baby mother, a trail of broken hearts in more than one country and is still single at a time in your life where you really want something more stable, it's time for you to take a serious break from relationships to work on you. OK! Maybe you don't need to go through all of that to take a break from relationships, maybe you just want to start over new and set some new goals and ideals for yourself and your future. If you're a man with big dreams and ambitions, but has yet to make a personal breakthrough that assures you that you're on the right path, it's even more important that you take a break from relationships right now! My biggest barometer for taking my most recent break wasn't necessarily my mishaps with women. I can honestly say that that was a big part of it, but I needed a break to assure myself that I was doing the necessary work I needed to be doing to live the life I want to live. If you spend time with your children, hold a job or have other heavy constraints on your time, it's very tempting to live a day-to-day robotic life where you're just doing what needs to be done, but are not inspired to do what you want to do. If you have chaos and confusion in your relationship, then that too is a huge distraction from not only your job, but it drains you and leaves you with very little left in the tank to put towards working towards your dreams. Taking a break is more about becoming aligned with your true self and your purpose than anything else.

The other important thing about your break is you get to prepare yourself for a new start when it comes to relationships. No one wants to be alone, but at the same time, if you've made a mess out of many of your past relationships, then it's time to hold yourself accountable to change a few things to avoid being stuck on stupid. A lot of men pretend they don't think about the huge mistakes they've made in relationships along the way, but I know I do. You'd like to forget about how you lied to her, how you slacked off at work and got fired, or how you missed the deadline for something important that you needed. You should use the data from these failures to create new avenues to success. You'll be able to see that the mistakes we make are usually all across the board and not only with women. Don't be the guy who thinks his only mistake was choosing the wrong woman, because if you look deeper, you'll see the same behavioral pattern being applied to a lot of different things in your life. We all make mistakes, but you should want to lead a life that has enough checks and balances in it to prevent a few of those mistakes from happening in the first place.

The wrong women

One of the biggest distractions outside of himself that any man will ever face in his life is the wrong woman. The wrong woman will feel really good in the beginning before she becomes a drain on your resources with nothing to give back to you to help you replenish your reserves. The wrong woman is the easiest woman to be with and the hardest one to get rid of. She usually comes with some good assets like good sex, constant availability, and financial stability that she always makes available to you. As long as you continue to use these resources of hers, she'll be right there, expecting your attention in return, but making your life miserable if you're not giving her what she feels she deserves from you. If you've had issues with these types of women, it means you're doing something to attract them. The perfect time to figure out how to change that pattern is when you take a break. Taking a break means you're going to have to close the door on her for good. Bye Felicia!

If you're like me, being single may seem hard to do because there are so many women around you who claim to be interested in you. It's important to know that many of those women are more interested in having your attention rather than being your ideal partner. You can't allow "illusory options" to cloud your judgment and prevent you from focusing on your life. For a lot of men, taking a break from relationships is the best way to get the time needed to reflect on their current predicament with women.

While on my break, I sat back to analyze all the women who revolved around me, and I didn't like how they all represented different mindsets and phases I'd been through. When I look at things from a different perspective, I empathize with the women whom I've misled in my very own quest for attention and sexual affection without commitment. For me, the mothers of my children represent a state of confusion and lack of self-confidence over the course of three years where I wasn't happy with the progress I was making towards my goals. Ex-girlfriends remind me of how selective I was in choosing who I wanted to be with. The women who are interested in me that I'm not interested in represent my ego because I keep them around as options. And then there are the ones who "got away" who represent the lack of confidence I had in myself that prevented me from wholeheartedly pursuing them. They're also "friends" who at any given moment can turn into friends with benefits. For men like me, this is regular. Many of us have a stockpile of "potentials" from the past and present that we keep as options just in case we don't find the one we really want soon enough. This is unacceptable behavior. You can't settle for women in the meantime before you move on to someone you truly want. That's a sign that you're afraid of being alone to yourself and a host of other potential issues.

Learning to trust yourself

I've learned that you won't ever trust a woman, no matter how trustworthy she is, if you don't trust your own decision making. Trusting yourself is going to be critical to your long-term and overall success in everything you do. Sometimes if you're used to listening to the echoes of others or even the suggestions of women who love you, you'll be conditioned to seeking approval or even second guessing your own decision-making process. If you find you're having these kinds of internal conflicts, your break time is a great time to address it and begin to work on yourself.

The right woman is going to need to be able to trust you, and she won't be able to do that if you appear to be uncertain about trusting your own decision making. A woman is likely to stay with you while you're busy making a mess out of your life, but please believe that you're going to have issues with her trusting you. When you still have the tendency to be flaky, indecisive and have a track record of making bad decisions, it's best to work on yourself on your own with as much help as you need. Women don't fix men, and they shouldn't be expected to. All you can ever ask for is a woman to be patient with you as you transition through different stages of your life, but she's not obligated to stick it through, especially if you're in a state of confusion.

It's not hard to recognize when a man doesn't trust himself. None of his answers will be solid, he'll change his mind often, he'll do things he said he wouldn't, he'll be back and forth in relationships with women he said he was finished with, he'll wait until the last possible moment to do things that should be high on his priority list, he'll allow others to make decisions for him, he rarely asserts himself—the list goes on. If this is you, you've got some serious work to do on your break. Building trust with yourself is a habitual behavior that takes time to develop. It requires you to listen to your intuition and trust in your "gut instincts." You're going to see that when you trust yourself, you'll be right most of the time.

Limiting your interactions with women

While on a break, it'll also be wise to limit the number of women you entertain. Women who like you will always find a way to be there to tell you everything is going to be OK (just lay your head on my pillow). But everything won't be OK if your life is stuck in the spin cycle. You'll keep doing the same shit over and over if you really don't stop to assess yourself and make necessary changes. For some of your fans, you can't do anything wrong; they're so forgiving. But they don't know the root of the problems you face and sometimes you don't either until the only person you have to face is yourself. The only person you need to be communicating with every day while you're on your break is yourself. If she likes you so much, she'll be there waiting for you after your break.

ELEMENTS OF A GOOD BREAK

Listening to yourself

Listening is a learned skill and listening to yourself is all about trusting yourself. You've got to be able to trust what you know within yourself. If you can't trust yourself, then that's a sign that you have more self-work to do. When you trust yourself, there will be a guiding voice that helps you in all your decisions. With enough experience, you learn not to listen to just anybody. In that case, you'd want to surround yourself with people you actually trust enough to listen to. Listen to only those who strongly believe in you and have the courage to correct you when you're wrong. In this case you want to surround yourself with mentors and advisors who have what you want. However, trusting yourself will quiet your need to ask others. It will also motivate you into taking action. It's not considered listening if you end up taking no action.

Perspective

Having perspective means you can step outside yourself to view things in someone else's shoes to understand why they feel the way they feel. If someone is going to be in your life forever, having the right perspective on them will help you manage your relationship with them for the better rather than constantly not understanding why you're at odds with them. You can't change others. The best you can hope for is that your changes can lead to a better, more profitable relationship between you two.

Accountability

This is perhaps the most important asset in your tool bag to becoming a better man. No matter how you do it, accountability all starts with owning up to your actions and behavior as well as how it affected others. Some men will say they're not responsible for how someone responded to their actions, but I tend to disagree. It's not that you're responsible for their reactions, but with the use of perspective, you empathize with how what you did made them feel. You've got to be able to admit your wrongdoings 100% of the time. Don't hide behind your excuses. And get this, be accountable without ever pointing a finger at the other person—no matter what they did to you. This separates the boys from the men. This can be applied across every spectrum of life.

Forgiveness

You've got to be able to forgive yourself before you forgive others. If you hold yourself accountable, you will get to a point where you actually see the effects of your mistakes. If it's a bad relationship, perhaps you finally see why she hates you so much right now. To truly forgive yourself for your own misbehavior means that you also are dealing with the root causes of why you did what you did. The goal is to repent—meaning to make changes and improvements that prevent you from ever doing what you did again. That is an incredible feat. If you can do that, then there's a great chance that you can also earn the forgiveness of the persons you have hurt.

7 Things You Must Do On Your Break

Everybody's break is different. Some men can take a break while still entertaining the possibilities of new relationships. But for this to work and not interfere with your personal development, you can't be on the phone or out on dates every day with every woman who likes you. Your time is to be devoted to your pursuits in life, not to maintaining or establishing connections with a woman you're interested in. No matter how strong you think you are, it will hinder you. When you've mastered being single you can learn to dedicate upwards of 80% of your focus on your purpose. This kind of focus can accelerate your personal growth as a man, but many men must learn to respect this sacred space they must take.

Incorporating these practices will help you dig deeper into yourself while on your break:

1. *Get naked with yourself*—Not literally, but figuratively. Strip yourself of all of your perceptions, all of your associations and all of the expectations that you and others have of you. Call a spade a spade, admit your wrongs, compliment your strengths, find your weaknesses and get help where you need help. Know yourself and know your truth. Accept yourself and reject the need to fit in or change for anyone.

2. *Face your fears*- When you face your fears, what you're telling yourself is that you believe in yourself much more than you believe that you will fail. It's often a mental thing because unless you're in danger, most fear is a matter of perception. Change your perception, and the fear disappears. Every doubt you continue to collect will become mental blockages so release every doubt. Never allow being "cautious" to keep you from pushing forward on something. Be willing to stand up in the face of every fear you have, one by one.

3. *Meditation*- Not the kind of meditation where you sit there to think about everything. But the kind where you think about nothing. That's hard to do if you've never done it before. If you're new to it, you'll be lucky if you can silence your mind for one whole minute. Try it and don't give up! The simplest goal to reach is to focus your mind on breathing in and out. When the mind strays, go back to

the breath. Keep going back to your breath. Then go other places. Before you go on YouTube University, first practice focusing on the breath. The goal isn't to incorporate anyone's style. It's to shut up your overactive mind.

4. *Affirming yourself-* The practice of affirmations is a very lucrative investment into yourself. If you've been through a lot in your life, if your confidence has been shaken by traumatic experiences, if your ex-girlfriend or ex-wife cheated on you, if you lost your job or lost an important loved one in your life, positive affirmations can help you build or rebuild a healthy state of mind to help you move forward. Sometimes we don't have the supporting cast we need around us to help with encouraging words and have to look to ourselves to be our biggest supporter. Affirmations can help you align yourself with your purpose, your vision, your dreams and desires when you make them a habitual thing you say every day. Don't miss a moment. Recite them like prayers—be hard on yourself about saying them every day and believing in them.

5. *Celibacy-* Sex is the easiest tool to captivate the attention of young boys when in actuality a proper rites of passage would include the prolonging of sexual contact until a boy understands his calling into manhood as well as all that it takes to fulfil his role and his purpose in life. This would begin before the boy understands his need for sexual intimacy. When boys or even girls get exposed to sex early, celibacy in times of evolution and growth becomes harder to do when it is a necessary component to transforming sexual energy into creative energy.

6. *Detox-* On my break, I struggled to detox and cleanse because my discipline wasn't on point. Eventually, I would buckle down and get serious about cleansing my body, though. I've always understood the importance of cleansing my body but never correlated it to my emotional being. Well, you must take charge in this, too. There are many of ways to detox the body, but the trick here is that through this process, you must also be releasing emotional toxins as well.

These negative emotions are thoughts and memories that don't feel good. So while you're cleansing is a great time to release these burdens and leave them in the past.

7. *Get in touch with your purpose—* There's a sense of self that a man gains when his life is purpose driven. This is something that men should seek, but instead many are seeking the approval of women. The woman for a man with purpose is a woman who understands that your mission in your life is more important to you than love. She is happy when you have lived the life you dreamed to live because she gets a man who is fully available to love her because he is satisfied with who is and what he has been called here to do. Understanding your purpose will eventually become your guiding light to knowing what to do and what not to do.

Don't sleep on the value you can bring to yourself when you take a real good break. The strategy here will only make you better if you dedicate yourself to improving every single facet that you can improve. It's more like a time for professional personal development if you take it seriously. The thing is, though, many men don't understand how serious it is to take this time to prepare themselves to go to higher levels in their lives because they are very caught up in often dysfunctional relationships. The worst thing to see is he who actually took a break from relationships, worked on himself, made personal breakthroughs while on break, but went right back to the same dysfunctional relationship patterns with women. Celibacy is the hardest physical part of the break, but it's not as hard as doing the personal work, developing a disciplined routine and following it.

Just so no one gets my message twisted: my goal is for men to realize that we play a bigger role in the success and demise of relationships than we're sometimes willing to admit, so we must better ourselves to get better results from relationships. An increased quality of life will be the first thing you notice when you've taken time to work on yourself without the interruptions of women and intimate relationships

SEPARATION IS A MUST

The break you take represents critical thinking, self-evaluation, introspection, elevation of consciousness and oneness with your purpose. Some men have to learn the hard way about the need to separate themselves from not just women, but anyone who doesn't fit into their lifestyle. Like it or not, relationships and even friendships that don't enrich your life must go, even if that means you must leave your environment. Since your breaks are about you, then you should seek to surround yourself with people who believe in your highest potential. For some people, it's hard to leave the people they've grown accustomed to, but success will often require for you to leave some things and people behind.

All of this is absolutely necessary to help you elevate to higher heights in your growth and development as a man. You will need to separate yourself and you must not be afraid to leave people and things behind when they no longer serve you. You especially need this space when your existing relationships are incompatible or worse, filled with chaos and confusion. What I want men who are in these turbulent relationships to know is that you don't have to accept this as the way things are, even if you've been told that "you're the reason why things are this way." If you truly change the way you think and operate, then it's only right that your relationships and your environment also reflect these new changes. Why stay where you're not growing? Why be around people who don't believe in you? Why work at a job you hate? When it's time to leave a situation, you must be serious about leaving it or risk being stuck there.

My most recent break represented a truth for me and my relationships with the mothers of my children. That truth was that the relationship door is now permanently closed, and we must begin to forge a new relationship based on co-parenting and friendship. In the past, before children, when I moved on, I moved on—whether women liked it or not. Now that I have moved on from relationships that included children, I will not allow my desire to be involved with my children become a tool to manipulate me. I tried it and it doesn't work for my life anymore. But it is what it is. I would prefer for things to be better between us, but until then, all of my calculations have indicated that it's in my best interest to stay away from this person, and I will listen to that. If you don't take your break seriously, no one else will. Allow no one to stay in your life who doesn't belong there. Have no mercy about leaving them behind when it's time to move on.

CLOSING THE DOOR

A huge part of taking a break from relationships is saying no and closing the door on the wrong women. If you're still conflicted about who's right for you, then you need to do some more self-reflection while on your break. There may be a lot of different reasons why you're still confused about who's right for you, but you must understand that this is no state of mind you want to dwell in. If you're confused about who the right woman is for you, you'll allow the wrong women to languish in your life, causing more confusion. There have been times in my life where literally every door to every past relationship, flirtation-ship and situation-ship was still left wide open.

A lot of men don't close the door on women because they like having options, but most of those options are what I like to call illusory options. The real truth is unless you're being cautious and taking your time to get to know her, if you haven't made a strong advance to be in a relationship with her, then you really don't want to be with her. If she's still hanging around after you've chosen not to be with her, then she's an option or maybe there for sex. Men don't marry their options. We marry the solution—the woman who we can't live without. Just be honest with yourself about who you keep around for booty calls and sexual rendezvous. But don't ever take risks to keep those women around. The ones who you've giving all that good loving to end up being the ones who have the hardest time letting go of you, so don't get caught up in your own lust.

THE CLOSE THE DOOR LIST

Cut buddies or friends with benefits

If she only comes over at night and you'd never be seen with her in the daytime, she has to go! I don't care if the sex is the greatest. If sex were that important to you, then you'd be in a relationship with her. Other than that, you're wasting your time. If you only see her when it's time for sex, then she's not actually a friend. She just has benefits.

Exes

She's an ex for a reason. If you keep her around with the expectation that one day she'll throw some butt in your direction in between new boyfriends, then you're second class. It's not fashionable to remain friends with exes, but I do understand that there are special cases where there is one ex that is actually a real friend many years after the relationship ended. But don't kid yourself, even she could be madly in love with you still and if it's the crazy kind of love then remaining in contact is going to cause problems

Baby mothers

She had a baby by you; she was stuck on you for a while. She played it off by acting like she hated you, but it was just misplaced emotions. She really does love you in her very own dysfunctional way. And you love her too, in your dysfunctional way. By now, you should know that it's the end of the road for you two, but just in case you're still sniffing fairy dust, here's a reminder—she's not the one! The sex with her is usually better than sex with someone new and the idea of waking up in the same house as your child always feels good, but she is what she is … your child's mother; not the woman you're with and certainly not someone who you feel helps you get better. If she can be a friend, be her friend, but if she needs your love, affection and attention, then make sure the door is shut tightly on her.

KEEPING THE DOOR SHUT!

Closing the door also means not allowing them to get back in. I had a partner who once told me that women are like mosquitos and that if there's a crack in the window, they'll find it and get back in. She was right because she was that same mosquito in my life sucking my blood. There are some clever women who know how to work their way back into your life if you don't know how to keep the door closed on them. These are the kinds who've studied you pretty well and know how to appeal to your senses. She may know where you hang out, have mutual friends with you and always finds her way back into your circle. It's even worse when you have a weakness for her because she's the infamous 'Devil in a Blue Dress' who is so hard to resist. A lot of times we feel it's OK to let her back in because we're not dating anyone right now and "it's just sex" with a familiar face. But it's not OK. It's not just sex to her; it's fuel for her ego and her sense of entitlement. The sooner you detach from her, the better off you'll be.

I was once the guy who never closed doors, so I know how easy it is to get caught up with a woman who has her mind and her heart set on you. You don't have to do much when a woman really has her intentions set on you, but if you've been weak and your weakness was how she found her way into your life, she's not going to be a fan of you being strong enough to now resist her. In these situations, it's like a game she plays to see what she can get you to do.

WILLPOWER TO SAY NO

The woman you can't close the door on represents your weakened willpower. Most men don't understand how their sex drive is intricately tied into their willpower. It's no coincidence that you have the best sex with the woman you just can't say no to. You never see it as life-threatening, but it is. Unfortunately, many men just don't see this woman for the threat that she actually is because she feels so good. It's all fun and games until you're stuck with her. Stuck with her as in she's pregnant and she's keeping it! Or even worse, she's pregnant again!

The joke is now on you because she wants to be stuck with you, even if you don't want to be stuck with her. If she didn't get pregnant the first time you had sex, then you had all the time before she got pregnant to stop, but you didn't because you couldn't say no. Sounds familiar? Well, that's one of my storylines. And I still have to work on my willpower, but I'll tell you this: I'll never be "stuck" with a woman I don't want to be with for one reason or the other.

A buddy of mine was married to a woman who loved him more than life itself. She was a good looking, good girl, but she was a push-over. After seven years together and two children, he was left yearning for something more exciting. He met a lady where he worked, and they kicked it off with a bang. Almost immediately, they were hooking up incessantly. She had him hooked. He described the sex as something dreams were made of. Sex with his wife couldn't compare to sex with her because she was a freak. He would go on and on and on about how this kind of loving was exactly what he needed in his life. She was in touch with her body and her sexuality because she had more experience with men than his wife did, and that's what he felt he was looking for. His wife would soon become a distant memory.

He got lost in the juices; lost in how many orgasms he could give her back to back, thinking it's all him; lost in the dirty talk and the raunchy sex. His sex life went from missionary-style every night to porn quality. This kind of sex was something he felt he could never get from his wife. So even though this represented the end of his marriage, it was exactly what he was yearning for. All the passionate sex with his mistress was also headed for a climactic end that he couldn't envision. To make a long story short, he began to despise his wife because she didn't want to end the marriage. The mistress ended up pregnant, but not before she told him the baby might not be his. The fed-up wife finally gave him a divorce (and other legal problems as well), and within a year, he went his separate way from them both, but not unscathed. If you ask him today, though, he'll tell you that he desperately wanted out of that marriage and that he was dying for sex as good as what he got from the other woman. Sometimes when your need for something is so great, you feel like you've reached heaven when that need is finally met. But most of us don't have the willpower to say no when that need that's being met is also causing chaos and confusion in our lives.

At the time this was happening to him, I couldn't understand two things 1) why was his need for sex that great and 2) why couldn't he just keep them both since his wife wasn't ready to leave him? I was certain that had he stayed with his wife that he'd eventually grow out of his need for the mistress and stay put with his family, but that was just my opinion. Many years later, I'd understand exactly what it felt like to be him as I dealt with my own situation with two women, where the sex with one was addictive and destructive while sex with the other one was infrequent and lacked excitement. There's something amazingly connective about raunchy sex that misleads you into thinking that the person you're doing it with might be the one. That's an illusory emotion; one you only feel before or during sex, but rarely after sex. Pay attention to your exciting sex life with the wrong woman and you'll see the other things around you starting to fall apart as well because it's never just about the sex. Look what happened to Tiger Woods.

You must possess the willpower to say no to what you must say no to, even when it feels good. And that's not just with sex but also relationships and critical decisions. If it feels good and it's wrong or detrimental, at some point you have to grow up and say "no, I can't do this anymore because it's not in my best interest for the long term." You must be able to trust your intuition to guide you away from getting caught up with women who you see no future with; sometimes she'll say no strings attached, but unless you're paying for sex, there'll be some strings attached somehow, some way. This is firsthand experience from a man who will now co-parent with someone who I just couldn't refuse sex from.

Closing the door on a woman who fucks you like a porn star is hard to do. In my case, I was able to close the door on her a few times, but I was never able to keep it closed, and when I let her back in, she wreaked havoc in my life all because of my lack of discipline. In your moments of self-reflection, look back at all the other things in your life that you didn't handle during that time, you'll see that the lack of willpower to close the door on her was also affecting other aspects of your life.

When your willpower is weak, the wrong women seek to stake their claim on this high-value fool (you). These women know that when you're at your strongest, they will be completely out of the picture. Your weak will is their only way to stay active in your life. She knows that you just don't know how strong you are as yet, and she feels that as soon as you get the strength you need, you'll actually move on to greener pastures without her. Sadly, these are the types who will get pregnant just to stick around. They often need major emotional healing from traumatic experiences in their lives, but instead, they hide their pain until it becomes too heavy a burden to carry. Unfortunately, these women are hard to save, so be prepared if one of these women end up having your child.

The longer you keep this woman around, the greater the potential that she'll despise you for wanting to move on. She'll see herself in your weakness and might try to keep you there until she can see herself as better than you. Unfortunately for her, that doesn't represent true growth nor love for self. This is a dangerous cycle to be caught up in with any woman, but like I said before, your willpower is what can eliminate this situation altogether or manage it. If you've already fallen for a situation like this, you'll still need your willpower to push you through the abyss. You'll need humility to accept the role that you played in this situation, but even then, you'll still have to close the door on her.

Having Standards

You gotta have standards you can live by and fall back on when you've deviated from them. It's like Christians who do a bunch of ungodly things that no one in their family approves of, but once they've snapped out of it, they come back to church to get saved. They do that because they regard what they learned in church to be their standard. Without standards, you may get caught up in a perpetual cycle of going back and forth between a rock and a hard place. Standards aren't always glorified, but when you have clear standards for relationships, love, marriage, dating, the rearing of children, etc., it's a foundation you can build upon that provides you with a level of comfort you can depend on. Standards are like rules to follow. Most people don't follow them exactly; however, those who use them as a guideline tend to be more successful according to the desired goal of those standards.

Standards for women

Sometimes as a man you have to have standards for the women he comes across. If the first time you met her, she gave you the green light to sleep with her, you have two options: 1) to sleep with her or 2) to hold her to a higher standard. Usually, it's hard for a woman to come back from this one, though. Most men are just going to think that she has low or no standards if she's ready for sex right away. I remember in my younger days, I used to think that if a girl gave it up on the first date, it was because my game was so good. I later learned it wasn't my game, it was her. Women have a multitude of reasons why they'll forget their standards for a man. I know for a fact that some women are just influenced by the wrong ideas and just weren't taught.

On the other hand, high standards don't necessary indicate high character. However, if you meet a woman with standards that she abides by, it makes it easier to have respect for her. There's really no coming back from sex on the first or second date unless you yourself manipulated her into sex. From my experiences with women, I can say that that's a familiar line I've heard many times from them. Many women have had premature sex with men who manipulated their way into their panties.

Her standards must align with her values. If you're observant, you'll know if she got her standards straight out of Steve Harvey's book. If that's the only place that she could find standards, I'm not going to knock her as long as she can be a good representative for the standards that she's following. As soon as the woman who says she's going to wait 90 days breaks that oath, men celebrate a victory! Most men enjoy a chase because it creates a sense of excitement. For some men, it's like a notch under our belts to get a woman to break her standards for us. It's a boost to the ego. Some men will pull out all the tricks in the bag to get a woman to break or lower her standard and then attempt to judge the woman against her standard for not holding it up. This is a narcissistic psychological game where a man literally makes a woman feel that she's not as worthy as she claims to be because she's not holding up her standard. With most men's objectives being so sleazy, I don't see how we could ever be in a position to judge when most men's goal is to have sex.

Standards for yourself

Men don't generally walk through the door broadcasting their standards because our standards are usually wrapped up in our presentation. The way you walk, the way you talk, the way you're dressed and all your mannerisms will be the telling story about your standards. You won't really have to have a conversation about it to make it clear to women. Later on, how you treat a woman will also define your standards. When a woman really likes you, she holds you to even higher standards because she doesn't want to lose value in your eyes.

A lot of guys will have women fooled by being well dressed and very chivalrous when they take a lady out for dinner at a nice restaurant. A woman with high standards will understand that that's just your representative doing a good job of a first impression. A lady of substance would be more impressed with how consistent you are at representing your seemingly high standards over time. When she's been taught well, she'll snuff you out if the first time you go all out for a date, but for the second date you want to Netflix and chill. That sends the message that you can't keep it up. A savvy woman will begin to sell your stocks right away.

One of the major reasons for taking a break from relationships is to figure things like this out for yourself. You can't be flipping and flopping while you're dating, so the best time to really get a handle on your own standards is when you're single and not seriously dating. A lot of men just don't set standards for themselves and thereby fail to hold the women they meet to high standards. Sometimes we're looking for a quick fix, but quick fixes generally aren't the ones will have your back in hard times.

Having standards for yourself will elevate you above your carnal nature that may tempt you to sleep with someone new who you know isn't your type. If her standards are lower than yours, by default you're lowering yours to accept from her whatever she's offering. Once you fall for the bait, she's got you and quite frankly, you can't redeem yourself after that. Your best bet is to cut it off, learn your lesson and move on.

THE HUNGER FOR MORE

Most men want the same thing, but highly evolved men want more. It's pretty common for us all to want the typical pretty woman with a great body. No matter how evolved you are, that's innate in all of us. Depending on where you're from, you may be wired to desire a different set of intangibles like wide hips or short/tall women, but everyone has their cultural programming to some degree. Many men have a physiological motor that drives them towards the women who they believe are of high value.

The role women play in relationships and society has changed so much in the last generation that you must know what standards you want your union to be rooted in. There's a tremendous amount of superficiality in today's world that is targeted at both sexes. Not everyone wants to admit that they're on that boat, but as you evolve as a man and align yourself closer to your standards, you begin to see through the smoke and mirrors and begin to desire for more than just the same woman, but the one that helps you become epic.

ACCOUNTABILITY
& MOVING ON

BEING ACCOUNTABLE IS ABOUT BEING willing to raise your hand and say, "Yes. I'm responsible for that." "I did that, and I'm aware that it hurt you." "I'm sorry, and I would like to work to make it right with you." You will have to swallow your pride to do this. But remember pride isn't a peacemaker nor a wealth builder. You will always gain when you choose to be accountable for the role you played and how it affects others, especially the women you've been with and the ones you have children with. Sometimes you can apologize to a woman who you hurt, and she chooses to never forgive you. As sad a situation as that is, it's out of your control once you've made amends. What's in your control is apologizing and making the necessary changes to prevent it from happening with her or anyone else again. You just remain humble and accept the fact that your actions led to things being like this. If the changes you've made aren't good enough to eventually make peace, then there's nothing more you can do.

With accountability, the hardest part will always be admitting that you offended someone you really care about and then sincerely apologizing. Men and women like to make excuses instead of apologies because sincere apologies will force you to deal with yourself instead of hinging everything on someone else. If you can get to the truth of the matter and come out and say it, the process begins to flow from there. The truth will always lead you to you. When you can say the ugly truth in the face of someone you care about without using it to demoralize them, then there is a chance that peace can crawl back into the picture.

STEP ONE — THE ADMISSION:

"I know you think I'm cheating on you with someone else, and I know you've been looking for evidence. I have been seeing someone else on the side. I lied about a lot of things before this, but the real truth is I'm only with you because of the baby, and I'm ready to move on."

Boom! That hurts! But if that's the truth, then it must be revealed. Men can't keep making a mess out of women because they weren't man enough to end it soon enough. Most women will know the truth before you speak it. Many men don't want to end relationships because they want to leave the door open so they can get back in at another stage in life. But it's important to fully admit the nature of why you've hurt someone so that way they can know it's you and not them.

STEP TWO — THE APOLOGY:

"I truly am sorry and I know this hurts because I know you care about me and you wanted this to work out for us and the children. I thought the right thing to do was to be with you because we have a child. But I was struggling to make it work because my heart wasn't in it. I didn't have the courage to end it early and I apologize that you were hurt because of that.

A true apology will hold you squarely accountable for your actions. It will also give the other person an opportunity to see that your actions are a result of actual problems you face within yourself rather than playing the blame game. When done like this, it's not just an apology. It's an inside view of the root cause of why you've done what you've done to hurt someone. It doesn't point fingers at the other person or blame them, even if they hurt you too. A true apology will lead you further into assessing what it is it that you really want for yourself, and it should always inspire you to make a better decision next time so you can avoid these kinds of situations altogether. This is where the men get separated from the boys because an evolved man will actually hold himself accountable for change, even if his apology comes at the end of a relationship. This is when you go back to the drawing board in hopes of creating a better outcome for yourself the next time around. This is where you finally learn the value of taking a break to know yourself and then go hard to achieve your goals.

DON'T BE UNAPOLOGETIC

It's not an apology if you don't mean it. It's not an apology if you came to apologize but ended up arguing and going back and forth with someone who you know you offended. That's your high pride that has you defending your excuses. This is not what accountability looks like. The man up portion is that even if they did you some wrong, you still must make peace with a sincere apology. That takes courage. Don't use what you don't like about them to stall your apology or create an argument that gives you another excuse for avoiding apologizing. Trying to convince someone you hurt that they hurt you too isn't how you make a sincere apology to them. No matter how much you grow and improve from a situation, you still can't dictate how someone receives it. You want someone who you pissed off to be calm and collective for you to apologize when you're aware that you are the reason they're upset? You might not get that, but that doesn't mean you can't still apologize and mean it.

A lot of men don't know the difference between their real self and their egos because we've been grossly misled into believing that our ego is who we truly are. But it's not. That ego will have a man hiding for decades from making a sincere apology when he knows he's dead wrong. That ego is what has men believing that they're "the man" and "it's my way or the highway." But that ego doesn't give a fuck about anyone; not your family, not your friends, not your children and not your future. The ego is a superficial representative that likes to show up when things are good to bask in the limelight but doesn't stick around through any hard times. The ego is that overactive mind that casts doubt on every situation and tries to create the impression that you are somehow more important than another.

Being unapologetic is likened to being a big sour puss, extremely full of yourself, unforgiving and self-serving. It's unfortunate that many men can't catch themselves in the middle of this high-level narcissism. The male ego is what fuels all of the bullshit that women use in their conquest to destroy a man's reputation when she's hurt. Some men drag their egos with them so long, and when they finally admit that they're wrong, it's after an embittered woman has spewed hate all over your life and onto your children because you couldn't see how you were hurting her with your behavior. This is the danger zone. You can die from this, and it doesn't necessarily mean death as in a coffin, but death as in not living for yourself because you're too consumed with superficial ideals of who you think you are and how others see you.

APOLOGY NOT ACCEPTED

Some of us men think that we're going to fix problems we created with women by just saying we're sorry. The thing about apologies is that they don't always mend broken hearts. Sorry is not always going to be good enough to bring harmony to a damaged relationship. And even in cases where you apologize and make noticeable changes, it still doesn't mean she's over it. But what sincere apologies and continued humility does is create a portal for healing and forgiveness that either party can retreat to when the burden of holding a grudge becomes too heavy to carry.

Men who have cheated on their monogamous partners and now have to bear through wicked games of control that she may play with the children only wish that they apologized sooner. If you cheated when you said you never would, she's no doubt going to be hurt. If she's an ultra-jealous and possessive woman, then she might want to kill you if your cheating embarrassed her and that may mean she takes a shot at destroying your reputation and ruining you financially. At this point, you will begin to see someone who truly doesn't care about you and is willing to make your life difficult because not only did you not give her the fantasy she dreamed of, but you went out of your way to add insult to injury by choosing to be with someone else.

Unforgiving women are unfortunately one of a man's greatest learning opportunities. Her rage has a way of showing you how much frustration some women have been dealt by the hands of men. After years of broken relationships and in many occasions emotional and physical abuse, it's no wonder why so many are willing to go to extreme measures to hurt you back. It shows you how conditional love can be and how important it is to be a man of your word despite what disappointments you may face with women. No matter how much leadership and independence women say they want, they'd still prefer to hold us to our word while their word is conditionally based on how they feel. It's just the way it is right now. You don't have to accept it, but if your behavior forces you in a position where you have to accept second class behavior from a woman, then being authentic with yourself and with women will be your only means of standing up and refusing second class behavior. If you hurt her, and she's on a mission to hurt you back, don't act like she should just get over it because you said you're sorry. And if you apologized as you moved and have sincerely made changes in your walk, she may not get the opportunity to witness that and may still hold a grudge. I'm not saying you've got to bare through second class behavior to win favor with a woman you've hurt, though. I'm just saying that many women are already so damaged that once they explode on you, you may not have the opportunity to pick up the pieces peacefully, yet you must remain humble, especially if you know you treated her wrongly.

WHEN COMMUNICATION IS NECESSARY

Women would like men to be tolerant of the games they play just because they're the mother of a man's child. But when she's consistently starting arguments and fights long after you have moved on, it's a sign that she's not ready to move on. During this time is when there's a higher probability of vindictive revenge games. It might be hard to ignore all the things she does to get your attention, but you must remind yourself that you had something to do with why she now behaves like this. If you have children, it means you must continue to see her, and you must continue to communicate with her. When children are involved, you're at a higher risk of getting caught up in the vicious cycles of games she may play to make you "feel her pain." It's very important to communicate efficiently with no ego. Continue to hold yourself accountable and take no offense, no matter what.

This kind of woman is convinced that since you did her wrong, you deserve no peace, but your peace of mind must remain a top priority for you. Children easily become pawns in revenge-fueled games that hurt people play. Some of the most demoralizing things get said and can happen within the span of a five-minute drop off or pick up of your child; women lose tempers and get emotionally unstable real quickly. Many know that they technically have the green light to cause you financial damage or get you thrown in jail. One of the hardest things to do is to walk away from someone who is calling you out of your name, threatening you or attempting to physically harm you. These interactions are dangerous for your spirit and even more dangerous for the children involved. But when egos flare, the only solution is to remove your ego and walk away. Even if you're big and bad, you still walk away from any arguments and confrontation because getting all upset won't change the person. If this becomes a reoccurring theme, then you should go through the court systems to ensure that there are clear and set expectations which you both must follow in regards to co-parenting your child. If she continues to violate, then she could end up in contempt of court if you report her. Don't take it easy on her if this is the type of person you're dealing with. It needs to be clear that you want and deserve peace. But peace will only come as a result of you choosing a new path to walk in your life. Don't expect peace to come from her forgiveness or even her moving on, it's only going to come from the actions you take that demonstrate that you truly are operating on a different level.

The best way to deal with communicating with the mother of your child who insists on making things difficult for you is to deal with everything through the courts; time sharing, child support, and court admissible text messaging and phone conversations. If she really wants to be on speaking terms with you, she'll make the necessary adjustments to communicate with you peacefully. This is where it becomes important not to accept second class behavior. Once you do, she may prefer to keep things this way as a means to get out of line with you to blow off some steam when she's had a rough day. That's not communication. That's somebody taking their pile of shit and throwing at you; duck.

SHE MUST BE ACCOUNTABLE, TOO

What I've learned from observing the behaviors of women whose feelings I've hurt is I've never been the source of all their problems, just like they weren't the source of mine. I hurt them, and in my self-work I had to find the answers to my behavior. Though it took me years to really hold myself accountable, the result of this level of accountability is the courage to deal with your own problems rather than pointing a finger at someone else. Under no circumstances are you ever so wrong that she has a free pass to cause mayhem in your life. A woman with class will allow you to be wrong if you are willing to admit it.

I truly don't believe there aren't any innocent parties, except for very few occasions. If you had a good woman who believed in you and you lied your way through that relationship, you're definitely responsible for lying. But I guarantee you that as unsuspecting as she appeared to be, she knew something was off about you. She's just as responsible for ignoring her intuition as you are for doing what you did; everyone's responsible for their ignorance, no matter how blissfully they bask in it. What makes apologies sincere is your ability to hold yourself accountable so you can identify the root of your problem and go fix that within yourself. When you dig deep within yourself, you will begin to see where you can improve as a man. If she chooses to behave as though she's not accountable for anything that she's done or her new spiteful behaviors, there's nothing you can do but continue to be accountable for the role you played. Trying to have any conversation where you're showing her her wrongs is a waste of energy.

FIX YOU FIRST AND BE ACCOUNTABLE TO YOU FIRST

A huge mistake that's easy to make is when you finally see where your problems are stemming from, that you run back to her to tell her how you now see the light and how you're ready to change for the better. At that moment where a man finally sees himself and chooses to be accountable for the hurt he caused a woman, he's still not yet a changed man. Even if it's a great big epiphany, you still have to put in the self-work on your own and become consistent at doing it.

We all want to share things that we've learned from our troubles, but we can't jump off the porch trying in a rush to redeem ourselves; early on we've only seen the light but have not walked in it yet. Reading a book gives you knowledge, but that knowledge is useless if you haven't applied it to your life. You must put yourself in a situation where you can consistently apply what you've learned. This is what transforms you, not the knowledge itself. When you've just realized your errors, you're not fit to go back to the woman whom you've mistreated asking for a second or third chance until you've demonstrated that you know how to operate differently. Many men are car salesmen who can sell a woman on how he's changed, but when he gets another chance, he ends up doing the same thing over again because he didn't give himself enough time to practice what he's learned.

This is where all the other components of taking a break can come in to assist you in the process of making changes. I never recommend making changes for a woman. I say make changes for your life. But when a man holds himself accountable for hurting a woman he loves, and he truly wants to be with, the opportunity to be with her again can sometimes be the fuel that drives his changes. I still say you must make them for yourself first because you must be able to live your changes yourself before you put yourself in a position where someone else is depending on you to be this new person you promised. Men who are used to being in a relationship with a woman will be challenged by a break from relationships, but it's the best thing he can do to focus on making lasting changes to the way he operates.

ACCOUNTABILITY FOR THE PAST, TOO

If you've been with a woman for a very long time, and you two made it through your young and dumb days, accountability means you're able to own up to your past behavior, too. If you truly do change, a woman who really does love you will forgive you, but she won't forget. Women bring up "old stuff" because they never forget how you made them feel. But a mature woman who has forgiven you and is proud of your new walk will encourage your new behavior rather than continuing to admonish you for the past.

Bottom line is that you can't come to the table only taking responsibility for what you did today and expect her to forget when you did the same thing last year or three years prior. If what you did last year and today are tied into the same root issues, then you may be missing something in your accountability toolkit. Don't embarrass yourself by saying, yeah, I was wrong, and I'm going to change, only to be doing the same thing again within a short span of time. You'll need to take another deep look at how you're holding yourself accountable to change and do something differently to ensure you get different results. In this case, holding yourself accountable is more than just saying you were wrong, but it includes pushing yourself to change bad habits that led to the behavior that you're attempting to change. If that means you change who you surround yourself with, then do it. It could also mean changing the music you listen to, where you hang out or creating a habit of reading new material. Just know that accountability is not just what you say vocally, but what you do and whether or not you're sticking to it.

The past can help you recognize what you're doing wrong today. It's as simple as looking at the results of what you're applying. You can't be full of apologies but continue to do the same things to hurt people you say you love. Women don't forget your past, so you shouldn't either. When you really hold yourself accountable, you're doing so in hopes of making changes to avoid repeating the past. Once you can move beyond repeating mistakes, then you can begin to move into the bracket of someone who has truly repented and no longer walks a path that hurts others. Then you eventually elevate to a level where your past cannot be used against you. That's where you want accountability to take you.

THE BLAME GAME

There's a stage that all of us go through when we're quick to say "it's not my fault." Maybe it wasn't, but did you do it? If the answer is yes, the solution is to start looking at the man in the mirror. There'll be a lot of reasons why you might want to start pointing fingers at her for what she did or what she didn't do, but that's a sign weakness. It's also a sign that you've been hurt pretty badly too when all you want to do is blame her for what you feel she has done to hurt you.

There are guys who've been cheated on that think that her cheating is a free pass to avoid being accountable for the role they played in why they got cheated on in the first place. My position is that you're still the man, the leader, and if she cheated on you, then something was off about your leadership. You obviously missed something on her scouting report, and you got exposed because you misjudged her or perhaps ignored a problem that you should have brought to the light. So since it hurt so bad, you chose the easy way out which was to blame her.

How long do you think a man can blame a woman for? What if she's the mother of your child and she has to be around—are you just

70

going to hate her until she tells you she's sorry? If that's what you're waiting on, you might die waiting for that apology because, in cases where the woman cheated, she likely moved on before she even left you. I understand that it hurts like hell when you've put a lot of trust into a relationship, and she burns you, but you must use it as fuel to be more accountable for not only the role you played but the role you allowed her to play in your movie. Your movie is your life, and you're always going to be the star and the director in it unless you choose to be the victim.

As a man, my position is that you're not allowed to blame her for anything. We see women pointing fingers at men all the time, and you must avoid doing the same. You have to put on your big boy pants and know when to take a loss. The more you obsess over an unfavorable situation, the more you attract it to you. Sometimes it's financial; sometimes it's emotional, and sometimes it's just your useless pride. Ultimately, a man blaming a woman for a failed relationship is a sign of a man who feels powerless. And don't get me wrong, I've heard it all about lying and cheating women who've devastated families with second class behavior, but I believe that there's something off about the man who all this happens to. The best thing he can do for his life is to go inside to find out where he can improve for the sake of avoiding this in the future. It can be an ugly mess when children are involved, but you still have to consider yourself the leader; hence, responsible for what has happened, too.

6 Do's & Don'ts to Help You in Your Process to Accountability

- Do: Be sincere in your apologies. You must remain humble for sure, but don't play anyone's "prove yourself to me" game.
- Don't: Keep apologizing over and over for the same thing to stay in good graces with her.
- Do: remain humble no matter what her disposition is. Walk away from abusive encounters, but still remain humble.
- Don't: Lower yourself to make her feel better about herself.
- Do: keep your word.

- Don't: Overcompensate her because you feel guilty. Sometimes when you've made mistakes you feel doing more for her will win her over, but it won't win a heart that's too damaged to forgive.

Two major don'ts to never do:

- *You don't owe her love.* "After all you've done, you should be worshipping me." No the heck you shouldn't be! You don't owe her your love no matter what you did wrong. That's not how love works, and that's not how forgiveness works either.
- *Don't accept disrespectful behavior.* Some women feel it's their birthright to give attitudes, curse outs, temper tantrums, excessive phone calls & text messages, etc. to show you how upset they are. If you have to take out a restraining order, do it. Don't allow this woman to get comfortable disrespecting you, especially if you have made efforts to show your sincerity moving forward.

Be real about moving on. Moving on sometimes means you cut all ties and all communication. Don't send her messages that make her feel like she's still a factor in your life. Don't arouse old feelings in her that will have her contacting you again. If she's been displaying disruptive behavior that she uses to gets your attention, you must move fast to stop this. Many men have the broken hearts of women dragging behind them because they feel too sorry for them to give them the royal cut off. Some of their intentions are to make it hard for you to move on, and the ones who are not fully over you will do this for as long as you allow it.

ATTRACT YOUR TYPE

YOUR TYPE SHOULD FIT YOUR desired lifestyle, and men need to be sure about the lifestyle they intend to live before looking to fit a woman in. Think about it—a lion doesn't pursue a lioness who lives a different lifestyle than him. She hunts for gazelle for them to eat. Imagine if she hunted for possums and brought it back. He'd be like WTF is this?

Many of my standards of performance I got from my upbringing; my father, my studies, my mentors as well as my experiences. I've learned that the standards of men are different, but I'll tell you this, when you're hitting your goals and performing at or above your standards, the woman you want will get in line and wait for you. And I'm talking about the one who you didn't have to lower your standards or compromise for. She's going to admire that you took a break from relationships to better yourself. She's going to love you more for all those things you worked on and improved while you sat out and watched your buddies stockpile all the ladies. High-value women recognize a man who isn't following all the usual trends. That's what a break does to you. After your break, you won't be jumping at just anyone trying to get your attention. Instead, who you want will be coming to you.

NOT MY TYPE

For many years as a photographer, I photographed thousands of beautiful women, but I never lost my composure over the women who came before my camera. During most of that time, I had a woman by my side whom I desired on many levels. I knew she was my type; she didn't look or behave anything like the women I photographed. Even with heavy exposure to those women and that lifestyle, I still desired the woman I had because I always refused to accept everyone else's standard of beauty, even as a model photographer. I consider women to be beautiful for many different attributes, even some of those I don't personally desire in my woman. It's important for a man to know what attributes he absolutely needs in the woman he chooses to build with. Once you know your type, you have to learn it so well that you can spot it in a crowd full of replicas. Your ability to reject women who are shape-shifting to get your commitment will serve you well on your journey and help you avoid the pitfalls of these women.

As a man, you fail a woman when you bring a woman into your world without the intention of keeping her in it. This includes engaging in sexual intercourse with women who you wouldn't want to build a family with. There are prostitutes who can satisfy your sexual need who are programmed to walk out of your life five minutes after sex with no regards to you ever again. But the average woman, even as independent and feminist-minded that she wants to be in today's terms will still form a physiological attachment to the man who leaves his DNA in her womb space via consensual sexual intercourse. It's risky business to expose yourself to women who you don't ultimately want to be with. Many men who take this risk, do so for the opportunity of good sex, and that often indicates a weakened willpower that is controlled by the overstimulation of sexual energies. There's hardly a mistake you can make with your ideal type, but opening up Pandora's Box with the wrong woman can be destructive to your soul.

AVOIDING THE WRONG TYPE

There was a time when I thought that I could just bring a woman into my lifestyle and she'd just adjust accordingly because she wanted to be with me. I always knew I was different from the typical guy, even when a woman didn't quite understand the extent of my differences. I'm not conventional by any means, and I haven't been since I was at least 19 years old. I don't celebrate Christmas; I don't believe in the so-called New Year, and I think Valentine's Day is a Roman-influenced fraud. I don't go to church; I don't follow a religion, and I don't take prescription meds. But I'm very much in touch with my spirit as well as the earth. My safest bet would always be someone who understands my transformation from someone who once followed these societal norms to someone who now views life differently. Major differences alone are enough to create serious dialogue between a man and a woman.

I went through a season in my life where I got this bright idea about experimenting with different types. But what in the world would I be doing with a woman who literally believed in everything I didn't?

Wasting time! Ancient texts says, "Can two walk together unless they be agreed?" The answer to that is no we can't!

When you take a break, you're supposed to look at all these ill-fated choices you made with women more carefully. Look at who worked for you, who didn't work and why. I found myself with a woman whom I knew wasn't a match for me, but I stayed in that situation because we were a sexual match. In the bedroom, she was exactly my type, and as long as we were having sex every day, she was happy as can be with me. We were sex addicts at the time and the more sex I had with her, the more distracted I was from the fact that sex was the only thing of substance we had between us. We'd listen to music, get high and fuck each other's brains out. She'd get up, and that's all she'd ever talk about—how good the sex was and how important it was for her to have this for a lifetime. I always knew it was just sex. She always knew it was just sex. But we both valued the sex over the fact that we weren't a match in any other category.

When you fall off your A-game, the illusions created as a result of sexual energies may seem real. My dipping self-confidence at the time and a bad diet kept me on and off her train for way longer than I care to admit, but I always knew that she wasn't close to being the one. My best friend would tell me over and over that I had to hit and run, not hit and stay because she wasn't close to being worth my time. But I wasn't comfortable with where my life was at the time, I made excuses why I couldn't pursue other women, and I continued to lay up with someone who was only interested in my penis being inside of her. She came easily; I never had to call her, never had to take her out, never brought her to my house. I never really cared to do much more than supply the sexual goods. I created a deadly soul tie with her that took three years to break.

Was she my type? No, but sexually she was exactly what I wanted. She was my sexual type, but she wasn't interested in my lifestyle. She wanted to convert me to fit her lifestyle to keep her sexually satisfied. I must admit that there were times where I thought about it because I too was addicted, but I would've never committed because it was all a byproduct of sex rather than a true connection that made each of us perfect for each other.

WHY WE FALL FOR THE WRONG TYPE

Men, we have to stop doing this to ourselves. Your holistic type will not arrive if you're still entertaining women who deep down inside you really don't want to be with. We've got to be able to make the necessary sacrifices to cut her off when we know she isn't the one. The good sex isn't worth the pain that comes with it when things fall apart—whether it be pain inflicted upon you, her or your children. When you're sexually involved with a woman whose lifestyle is in direct opposition to yours, you must move faster to close the door on her. You denying yourself will allow for tremendous growth in your spirit.

Many relationships can't stand the test of time without sex because abstaining from sex will bring the truth of the relationship center stage. The truth is your will was weak, and you weren't strong enough to break away from her. The truth is that you both get lost in sex or whatever other guilty pleasure you shared, but you don't agree well enough to be together. Don't blame her! It's hard to find a man for some women, so if the sex was good and she hung on to you without having to do much for you, she did so because it was a good deal for her. She too knew it wasn't going to last forever, but since you were weak, she took it upon herself to enjoy the ride while you allowed it and while you were dishing it out.

The wrong type is a chameleon. She gives you the illusion that she's right for you because she adapts to most situations well enough for you not to notice that isn't her true color. Her adaptations to please you could be in the area of sex; it could be food, money or convenience. Men do this same shape-shifting to lure women in, too. Sometimes we're not conscious enough to recognize just how wrong a woman is for us, but if you're ever confused about this, just look at the results you've been getting since this woman has been playing a role in your life. Are you happier, healthier, richer, more focused and determined? Keep notes of that. The most humbling part of choosing the wrong woman is when you're able to identify what needs or what specific weaknesses of yours brought her into your life. You begin to rise above these types of women when you begin the process of healing these shortcomings that led you to her and others like her in the first place.

YOUR IDEAL TYPE

All men have an idea of their type. Sometimes we get a little fantastical with it in hopes of getting a unicorn, but if you're a down to earth man, you should know what you're willing to accept and what you must pass on. A lot of guys need only have that self-confidence it takes to say no to the ones they need to pass on and go after who they really want. If you don't know your type, then self-reflection while on your break is definitely going to help. You can't keep all these "almost your type" women around who cloud your vision and expect to ever see your type in the midst of all of them.

Who you want must be a real woman of substance who, by the means of continued conversation and interaction, elevates herself to the top of your list. She can't be a fictional character you've never seen before. I've met many men who've never gotten the woman they wanted because what they want is unrealistic. I'm not the one to tell any man he can't have a Beyoncé, but the Beyoncé we see isn't real. If you think that's who you need in your life, then you need to check your motive. Do you want a woman to help you build your family and community or do you want someone to be posting pictures on Instagram with? If the woman you strive for is based on artificial imagery, then you may have a long road to travel before true happiness finds you, if it ever does.

YOUR TYPE SHOULD FIT YOUR LIFESTYLE

Your type is always going to be an inside-outside combo. Most men want a pretty friend: a good looking woman who he can talk to about anything. Most men will drop everyone on their roster for an opportunity with a pretty friend. Other men want more like a pretty friend with a big butt (me). And some men are happy with an average looking friend with a big butt. The key attribute is friend (not a big butt). Every man's ideal type is a good looking woman he can talk to who also complements his ideal lifestyle. Good looking is, of course, determined by his cultural perspective of beauty.

These are what I call physiological needs that attract you to your ideal woman subconsciously. Beyond that, your type should fit your lifestyle, your culture, your religion, etc. She doesn't necessarily have to fit every bracket, but successful relationships all share some of the same key ingredients like lifestyle goals, the way you want to rear children, where you want to live, etc. It scares the piss out of me to think that I'd sit down for dinner with my wife, and I'm eating broccoli, potatoes, and lentils, and she's eating broccoli, potatoes, and steak. But that's me because I don't eat meat. Everybody has their hang-ups, and you have a right to have yours. Just don't allow those hang-ups to ruin your chances with someone who is otherwise 100% your type.

Be real about what you want for yourself. Your break should force you into that. Don't accept less, especially when what you want is based on who you are rather than superficial stereotypes. If she's not OK with what you want for the now and the future, then smile with her as you move along because she's not the one. You just have to be real about it and not settle for the freak of the week. If you want to grow food in the mountains somewhere, your ideal woman wants to do that with you. If you want to be famous, then your ideal woman would be in agreement with that. When the initial decision to be with a woman is based on the fact that you two are in agreement with the lifestyle you want to live, it becomes easier to solve problems that may arise between you two.

FROM THE SUPERFICIAL TYPE TO THE BENEFICIAL TYPE

Sometimes when you take a good break, your type will change to fit your new state of mind. If you've evolved from the self-work you did on your break, you should factor in those changes and keep in mind that you may need someone a little different than what you previously liked. That's what dating helps you to do after your break. The thing is now that you've taken a break and upped your value, you've got to be a little more selective with who you pursue. Your goal isn't just to have a good time or have sex; instead, you want to make a big splash with someone you know is attractive and wants what you want. There are different reasons to be attracted to a woman, but you know it's really special when you feel like she can be your wife.

The self-work that you've done will help you to see why the types that you chose before are no longer suitable for your needs, and you should get used to passing up easy opportunities for sex and comfort with women you know don't fit you. In the beginning, it'll be hard to say no, but once you can look yourself squarely in the eye and stay committed to your process of self-improvement, it gets easier to resist the temptations of the wrong women.

If your type was the prettiest girl with the longest hair and hottest body, but with that type you weren't able to manifest a happy and functional relationship, then no matter how much you're physically attracted to her, you can't go back down that road with that type. This is hard to do because if your type is usually the most attractive, it'll be hard to resist her pull. Only when you have done the self-work and have committed yourself to attracting a woman who complements your lifestyle will you be entirely satisfied with the decision. The goal is someone who fits you now and is committed to being there by your side later.

CHANGE YOUR ROUTINE

The best way to avoid getting the same results is to avoid doing the same things. If you met this kind of woman at nightclubs, then you should avoid nightclubs. If you met her at your job, then you should stop dating people you work with. At some point you must take charge of your own elevation, but only if you can take the time to identify your weak points and work to improve them. The real process here is you going from good to great, and that process is heavily dependent on the little things and the major things you decide to do differently in your life. When you're not pleased with the results you've been getting, you must become vigilant about making changes that will yield better results for your life. You don't need a therapist to tell you this. And even though men know this, some drag their feet making the necessary adjustments they need to make because they lack the discipline needed to follow it through and no one around them cares enough about seeing them truly do for themselves.

The only reason you're changing your type is so you can attract someone who will support what you strive to accomplish in life. It's easier when you're both in agreement that what's best for you is best for the whole family. If everyone else you were involved with couldn't help you become a better man for whatever reason, then this is finally the time to make it a priority to make sure that the next woman you're with is someone who has enough in her tank to offer encouragement and support for you along your path, no matter how she feels about your given path. This time around, you'll have to avoid women who want to fight for all your attention at the expense of your life's work.

High value women know the value of your success, and despite some of their emotional needs sometimes going unmet, they are willing to put your success first because you have shown them and they know it's what's best for the family. You not only want to be happy with the woman you choose, but you must also be happy with the life you choose to create for yourself long before she comes along.

A change of routine means you're throwing out all the learned behavior on approaching women and choosing to do things differently. The change of routine I speak of includes changing common routine things like going to a different Wal-Mart than the one you always go to; changing where you and your buddies hang out; choosing to have lunch with her for a first date rather than dinner and more. The new routine needs to be more goal-orientated. Meaning the places you go to have purpose in your life at that moment. You don't ever want to go where you don't belong. It's important to get to a point in your life where you enjoy the life you live so much that everyone you meet along this path understands you more because they get to see you as you do what you're passionate about. Your routine is supposed to be all about you. Allow yourself to become consistent at operating within it before you add women to it. It's important to find your groove for as long as possible before you begin spending time with women again.

Many men have been conditioned to rush things with a woman if they really like them. On the other hand, women tend to take things slow if they like you more than they like anyone else. We're so used to giving up our time to whoever needs it, but Heart On Break is about rewiring you to think differently. When you're single and you're on your break, you need to be able to spend upwards of 80% of your available free time working towards you life's mission. What that looks like is less social media, less hanging out with people who can't help you, less doing for others, etc. all in the name of spending more time working on your purpose. If men only knew that real love and admiration from a woman comes after she's witnessed them fulfil their life's purpose in one capacity or another. We are rarely focused on our missions because of the amount of distractions we face in life. Women and children will take up a tremendous amount of time. Working to accomplish your purpose requires time and dedication that one must put first. Most men struggle putting themselves first, but to be successful at launching your life, you need to be so focused on doing the necessary work that it takes over your life.

CHEMISTRY & COMPATIBILITY

Good chemistry with a woman is something you feel between you two almost immediately. It's something that's undeniable, and it creates secretions of hormones in your body that pull you in closer and closer to her no matter how far away she may be. This is perhaps one of the greatest human feelings ever—especially when this kind of energy is being exchanged between two people who are completely open to receive the energies they are sending to each other. Good chemistry is sure to inspire good sex, but good sex, even with a woman you have great chemistry with, can still turn into a sour point if you later find that you're not compatible. Chemistry is what you feel, while compatibility is how well you two can mesh together.

Compatibility is something that unravels itself as a byproduct of time spent. While chemistry can be felt almost immediately, determining compatibility may take some time. When compatibility and chemistry align themselves, it'll feel like magic. You two will always want to be close to each other, but the best part would be how well you find that you two are agreeing. There'll be a lot of, "me, too's" and "I feel the same way, too's" when you talk and it'll seem like you can talk for hours. You'll find she's the one who wants to do what you want to do and wants to go wherever you go. Most men who have had good chemistry with a very compatible woman will do their best to hold on to women who we share this kind of connection with.

If you've failed at relationships before your break and were never able to experience how good it feels to have good chemistry and compatibility with a woman, your radar may not be programmed for this. Many men, like myself at one point, have gotten used to shutting down perfectly good women who fit them well in favor of the "Devil in a Blue Dress" who is usually all about her sex appeal and a high profile lifestyle (entitlement). After your break, you can't be weak for this anymore. Falling for the same type that has proven herself to be no good for your long-term success is not allowed. If you like superficial women, it's often a reflection of superficiality within you. The best woman is the woman who impacts your life positively. If you've never given her the time of day before, after your break will be the perfect time to start talking to her more.

YOU ATTRACT WHAT YOU VIBRATE

I'll keep reminding you that you get what you spend the most time thinking about. I remember seeing the end of some relationships before they ever started, and it's no coincidence that they were over within a short period; simply because of that thought process. There was also a time when all I cared about was how good the sex was going to be. During that time, I had great sex with all the partners I had. I got exactly what I wanted because most of what I was looking for in any given relationship at that time was great sex. When I analyzed the results of this way of thinking, it became clear that I wasn't going to get more out of relationships because I wanted good sex more than anything else in the relationship. I attracted exactly what I spent the most time thinking about—sex.

Years later, I still want good sex in a relationship, but I've learned how to enjoy getting to know a woman without the immediate need to insert my penis in her after she's laughed at three of my jokes. I got what I wanted for a long time, so it's only right that a change in the way I do things required me to work on manifesting other things in a relationship like exploring our compatibility rather than trying to figure out if she'd be good in bed. Good sex tends to happen if there's good chemistry. But most men rush into sex as soon as they get the green light and don't take enough time to build chemistry. If there is good chemistry and conversation, you should be looking to continue that process until you both are mutually interested in being with each other. Rushing into sex, as glorious as it may seem, is almost always a set up for drama scenes straight out of a lifetime movie. It's a process to get to the point where you can say no to your body's intense desire for sex. Your break is your ideal time to transmute all that built up sexual energy into discipline and courage to pursue your life's biggest dreams.

After your break, you want to be vibrating at a higher frequency; one where you are consciously aware of the wrong women and you choose to avoid them—even if sex is easy. If you just consider that whoever you attract could be the opposing reflection of you, then you'll see that this selection will tell a lot about where you are in your current state of being. I've had to learn to look past all the women with potential to make room for she who is heading in the same direction as I am. A lot of men shy away from this truth, but the fact will still remain that who you end up with is a reflection of you, so take your time to build or rebuild yourself to attract someone who represents this new way of life you intend on pursuing. You have to be sure of what you want before you'll attract someone who wants the same thing as you do.

BREAKING UNHEALTHY
SOUL TIES

MEN LOVE TO PRETEND THAT they can walk into a woman's life and walk out with no repercussions on them. That may be the case for some of the cold-blooded types. But realistically speaking, we create soul ties with women that can stay with us for a long time, too. A soul tie is a physical, spiritual or emotional bond that connects you to someone in ways you just can't make rational reasoning out of. A lot of men don't realize that some of these ties need to be broken to fully move on. Special connections with high-value women should always have a place in your heart, but they should never hold you hostage and keep you from being happy with someone else once the relationship has dissolved.

Some men are no different from women when it comes to maintaining bonds from their past relationships. It's been said that women carry the DNA of men who've released semen in them forever more. I'm not sure how true that is, but I can say that the women I've encountered who have slept with more men were generally more confused and emotionally combustible. But I've also met many women who went through their "ho'" stage" and came out with a better understanding of themselves. Most men don't realize when they're stuck on someone and are in denial about it. Some of us are too busy putting up a shield to our true emotions that we don't know how to recognize that we're still stuck on someone from our past.

There was a time where if I found too many similarities to my old relationship in a new one I would literally sabotage everything because

I feared it would turn out like the last situation. That's when you know you're not over someone because you're still running from them even after you've moved on. Don't front about it; if this is the case, then she's still on your mind heavy.

Many men are unknowingly ruining every new relationship they start because they're still connected to a woman they haven't moved on from. If you still have your guard up or are fearful that someone new will do you wrong like the last person did, then you've got some ties you need to break. Sometimes you're going to have to be real with yourself to know whether it's that you don't want someone new to treat you better than that person you're still connected to did, or if it's that you're still hurt and haven't fully recovered. This can be incredibly complex to deal with, but it's not that hard to recognize. If you've been unsuccessful in all your relationships after "her" and you're still constantly referencing her—negatively or positively, that's a sign that you haven't moved on. Men don't like to be real about this. If you find that this is you, then you must dig a little deeper on your break to assess why you're still connected to her and change the behaviors you still exhibit that are keeping you connected to this person.

RECOGNIZING THOSE SOUL TIES

How many times have you attempted to go back to an ex? You find faults in the new person, and you end up at the doorstep of she who you still have a very strong connection to. It floats her ego to see you begging for her again, but the truth is she's not over you either, even if she has dated other men. Every time I hear that story, I think to myself that could never be me. But it has been me. I've come back as many as three times to two different women. You couldn't tell me then that I had soul ties to them, but the proof is in the pudding.

What you're doing when you keep going back to her is re-establishing that soul tie. Your relationship with her may never actually improve for the better, but the bond you guys share intensifies dramatically each time you get back together and so do the problems you have.

Each time I went back, I was always feeding my mind with some pie in the sky story to justify some logical explanation as to why I was doing this again with her. Every story I fed myself was egotistical and never addressed the real issues I had with myself and her. Every time I went back, subconsciously I knew no real progress had been made to better things between her and me. I cowardly just tried to forget about the past and hoped for a better future this time around. I realize now that I really couldn't help myself. Everything about us made absolutely no sense, but the connection was stronger than logic.

That's when a woman knows she's got you. If you mistreated her and she mistreated you as well, subconsciously she knows that she's no better than you are, but if you're the one coming back to her, it now seems like she's the one who holds the power to your happiness—especially if there are children involved. Since you wanted her back, even if it was rooted in seeing your children or whatever offer you made her, be prepared to have that power you've given to her used against you. In some cases, it should be used against you to humble you and teach you how important it is to deal with yourself before taking women for roller coaster rides. It wasn't until I was dragged by my face on the concrete pavement that I realized I could not under any circumstances re-establish this kind of soul tie again.

Unhealthy soul ties have a way of making bad decisions feel OK, even if both parties are fully aware that they shouldn't be dealing with each other again. For me, what I should've been doing was dealing with myself to break the connection to her rather than thinking that establishing a new relationship with her again was going to finally bring us happiness as a couple. From my experiences of going back, it's always been me not recognizing the soul tie until the soul tie has strung me out. Soul ties aren't just physical connections established from sexual intimacy. Many times, they are also highly emotional; rooted in your self-value, happiness, sadness, pain, jealousy, children, disappointment, etc. Sometimes that person you're still connected to was your first love; the first woman not named Mom who you really loved, your favorite person to talk to; the mother of your first child; your high school sweetheart; the woman who believed in your dreams; the woman who gave the most to you; the one you really saw yourself with, etc. We tend to feel like these kinds of connections are the ones we want to keep forever, even when they've taken a turn towards dysfunction.

These are your heart's memories that are the hardest to forget. Like I mentioned in the close the door chapter, many men leave the door open because of the illusion of having an option to go back to if or when things in their present relationships go bad. Other times we leave the door open because the breakup "wasn't so bad," or "we still love each other." But if you're not together right now, then that should be the biggest sign that you must pay attention to, not how you feel about the past or the potential of the future. If you ever learn the value of your emotions, then you'll always have happy thoughts about some of these women you had dynamic connections to, but remember that when it doesn't work, you should never force it. There are far too many people who think it's OK to move on without moving on, and it's totally unfair to your new partner to be constantly compared or referenced to an ex who you're truly not over.

I met a woman recently, who no matter what conversation we were having, she always found a way to bring up her ex. I didn't want to seem like a hater by telling her to shut the hell up about this guy, but at every moment she had an opportunity to talk about him, she would. She was still very much connected to him, so I red flagged her and told her to go be with him because she's apparently not over him. I meant it, too because I left her alone, thereafter. What I noticed was in her mind, she felt she could easily move on, providing the right guy came along. But as I listened to her tell me about guy after guy who came along after him, there was one reoccurring theme—she was comparing them all to him. She felt absolutely sure that he was the one for her, even though he left her. Another red flag about her was that this guy was nearly ten years her junior. When he left, he didn't close the door on her, and that gave her hope for a future with him. The effect that had on her was that she began sabotaging, over analyzing and criticizing the men she'd meet because she felt that the one she really loved would eventually come back to her. She wasn't really willing to take anyone else seriously. She just entertained them to float her ego. My conversations with her gave me so much perspective on the doors that I kept open in the past. I had never considered them from a woman's perspective. This lesson taught me the duality of closing the door. I never considered that the women whom I kept the door open for were potentially passing up on good guys for the possibility of being with me again.

Breaking the ties for good

Healing can't take place if you don't know you need to be healed. I can honestly say that I've been that person who was clueless about the impact these soul ties were having on my life. Within a four-year span, I met wonderful women whom I liked and enjoyed, but I kept going back to unhealthy relationships with the women I had the strongest ties to. I wasn't really in it for my own happiness; I was addicted to the process of going back and forth. If anyone new came along, I would quickly and easily detach myself from them without explaining myself. I couldn't stay connected to anyone new because somewhere in my psyche I didn't want to break my existing ties.

My strongest soul tie to date was one built off a sexual connection. When we were apart, she would call me to tell me that she's scared of moving on because she couldn't imagine life without sex like the sex we had. In this relationship, sex was the god. Without it, we drifted. With plenty of sex, we were almost inseparable. But everything else about the relationship was a mess. We agreed on nothing and even though I always knew this, I valued the sex as much as she did and was hypnotized by it. I got a high from satisfying her. I had never met anyone so sexually expressive or so in need of my affection. She wanted me to live inside of her, and I naively felt honored.

Breaking a connection like this started with having the willpower to say no to sex and attempting to find more ties that bind us together. But as we had less sex, more problems arose, problems that we always knew we had. With less sex came threats of finding someone else to show her affection. Eventually, without sex, she would become so erratic, so emotionally combustible that it threatened my safety. What's ironic is that I knew all of this from my first attempt to break the tie, but back then I just couldn't prevent myself going back to her again. Things came to an ugly end, where I literally had to retreat and cut off all forms of communications. The tie for me is now broken, but apparently, it wasn't meant to happen in a peaceful manner.

I know it was a physical soul tie that bonded us together because even after the ugliness of everything she still believed that we must continue a sexual relationship. It's been made very clear to me now that if I were to fall into that situation again, I might not make it out alive. Either that or my freedom would be limited. I enjoyed the sex as much as she did, but I guess it needed a dramatic ending for me to finally say, "No. I'm never doing this with you again. Ever!"

I say, "You don't' have to apologize for being imperfect." I believe in that because no one is perfect. If you need someone to apologize for every mistake they make to have a healthy relationship with them, then you're probably a narcissist. Not everyone understands the fullness of the consequences of their actions. But I do feel you should apologize to someone you've hurt, even if it were unintentional. I was a little naïve about a lot of things when I created some of these bonds with women. I never understood the physiological effects that sex, good sex at that, had on women. And I certainly wasn't aware of its effects on myself, also. I never thought I'd risk so much just for sex. I never thought that my addiction to a bad situation was such a major indication of my need to work on myself as a man. In a perfect world, we all get to walk away from the accident scene unharmed and unaffected, but this isn't a perfect world. Both parties have to walk away accountable for the role they played. Sometimes you think you're in better shape than you appear to be in the aftermath of things, but like in all major accidents, as time goes by and the adrenaline calms down, the pain begins to set in.

In the early days, I wanted desperately for her to leave me alone because my willpower was too weak to fully close the door on her myself. I had to become empathetic about the emotional trauma she felt from me not making her the one, for not wanting to marry her, for getting her pregnant (on more than one occasion, but only having one child), for never desiring a relationship with her until she got pregnant, for having sex with her and leaving as often as I did, for never seeing a future with her. These were all negative soul ties that she associated with me, and as we kept on being intimate, the pain of them grew stronger.

Soul ties will make you do some crazy things, and it's important to know that when you find yourself making a ridiculous amount of irrational mistakes you can't explain, it's time to stop. Just stop everything because your livelihood is in danger if you continue this behavior. Even if you have to lose a job or if it costs you more money than you have to pay, just stop. Stop before you put yourself in a hole you can't climb out of. The stress of a dysfunctional relationship can have debilitating effects on your body, and if you're not living a healthy lifestyle, it will add to the list of things that are literally making you sick.

Sometimes you have to escape from an unhealthy soul tie like a runaway slave. In this quest for freedom, you must be willing to lose all that you think you have to be free. Ultimately, this book is all about self-reflection. One must be able to see how their own behavior, specifically, served as a catalyst for a series of events involving someone else. The unhealthiest of soul ties have a guilty pleasure sensation that you feel about it when you're in the thick of it. You enjoy the feeling intensely, but eventually, you begin to see that results aren't helping you win in life. That's when you begin to have the courage to say no and distance yourself from these ties that are nothing but lessons you must learn as you move on.

COMMITTED TO
HEALTHY LIVING

IF YOU'RE GOING TO EVER maintain long-term success in anything, your health will be the major component to you being able to do so. We live in a fast-food nation where sickness is coming as fast as the food is. Even what we consider to be healthy is some form of processed food that would never be as nutritious as the fresh version. Fresh food, grown organically and sustainably is a critical fuel for the human body. What you eat is always going to play a role in how you feel and how you behave, whether you are aware of it or not. It doesn't matter how good your genetics are; today there are thousands of harmful additives in the food you eat, the air you breathe, the water you drink and all of the products you apply to your skin that slowly poison you as well as alter your state of mind. Food is and will always be of critical importance to the long-term survival of man. The issue today is, does man even know anymore how to feed himself food that helps him thrive on the planet?

Men have been influenced to eat the worst diets and live some of the highest risk lifestyles yet beat their chests like the king of the jungle while their minds and bodies are rapidly deteriorating. If you're the typical American, who wakes up to a big breakfast filled with meats and starch, eats a late greasy lunch then another huge greasy dinner late at night, then you need to count yourself in for every sickness. You might be fine now, but sooner or later one of the big time lifestyle diseases is coming for you. Doesn't matter how good your genetics are, today's low-quality food is designed to leave you deficient to the point where sickness and disease become inevitable. Think it's a game if you want to, this food system is filled with nutritionally voided foods masquerading as "fresh" and "healthy."

CHOOSING FOODS AS MEDICINE

Healthy eating is now as trendy as ever, but most men are still reluctant to make permanent changes to the way they eat. A lot of men think they can just go to the gym and work off all that heart slowing food they keep eating when that's really only one part of the solution. Sure, going to the gym consistently will help you look good when your diet is everything out of a drive through, but it won't work off what's happening inside your body. Not everyone who gets heart disease or diabetes is going to be obviously obese. What men must realize is that weak food is for the weak man. The present food system that you live in produces inferior food for you to consume. If you eat it or have eaten it, you have supported it. Your dependence on it or forms of it shows you have no real knowledge of how to feed yourself and heal yourself in cases of emergency. Real food seems so far away from most people today. Many of us grew up on some good home cooking that had a little bit of everything good and bad for you in it. We've grown to love our comfort fried foods, junk foods, and fast foods. Many others grew up in inner cities where virtually no retail outlets sold any fresh fruits and vegetables. These neighborhoods are called food deserts, and they're systematically designed to feed the people in those communities low to no nutrition processed foods containing traces of actual nutrition with some containing a cocktail of fortified synthetic vitamin additives. Other than that, all these processed foods are made of a mixture of sugar, corn, wheat, soy, and cheap oil. A child will not function efficiently for very long on a diet that is lacking in essential vitamins and minerals, but a huge percentage of the average person's diet in America is composed of these kinds of low-nutrient processed foods. Eventually, those children growing up in the food deserts will begin to lose the ability to stay focused and dedicated in school. Those areas usually have a correspondingly high rate of high school dropouts, crime, and poverty. These men, women, and children are the least bit aware of the simple fact of their lives: they are malnourished and undernourished.

It's 2016, and we still have large tracts of the population who eat aimlessly. The food they eat is chosen for them while they think that they're choosing what they eat. This is my wake up call to you to realize that you can choose something that's better for you. The choice is going to be to change the way you look at food and begin to consciously consume foods that are nutritious and healing to your body. You don't want to be the guy who's forced to change his diet by the dire warning of a doctor, but because you've spent so much time eating the wrong foods, eating right is a huge challenge for you. It's time everyone woke up to the choices they have because when it comes to food, every fiber of food you put in your body has to be produced somewhere, and the more you purchase, the more that will be produced for you and others.

The re-education process must begin when it comes to what we think we know about food and how it is produced. We live in a country where there are so many different ideals on what healthy is that it's safe to say that as a whole we're truly confused about what eating healthy truly is. The many different directions that "healthy" has created has only added to the confusion of what healthy truly is. Healthy for men has a lot of different factors that play into it, however, no matter how healthy your physician says that you are, your health is continually fading as long as you continue to consume certain foods like red meat and practice certain behaviors like worrying and stressing yourself.

WHAT MEN CALL HEALTHY

Men tend to be the last ones to go to the doctor for check-ups, so if we were to ever find something wrong, we would literally be racing against the clock to fix it in time. I'm in that number because I have health insurance, and I'm still reluctant to go to the doctor. Most men don't trust doctors and end up suffering tremendously from not paying closer attention to their health. I like to say that your health index is the best indicator of your wealth index. The healthier you are, the higher your vibration is and the more potential you have to live a happy and fulfilled life. If you're not as healthy as you know you can be, the foods you choose to eat can be the hidden culprit in why you face many health problems.

A seemingly healthy friend of mine was going through one of the most turbulent times in his life that included a divorce from his wife and separation from their two children. The process was an emotional roller coaster that had outsiders wondering if he was crazy or losing his mind. A year later, he was diagnosed with chronic kidney disease, and everything started to make sense regarding his behavior. While making a royal mess out of his family life, his kidneys were also failing him. When he was diagnosed, it proved how fragile a man's state of mind and body can be when dealing with large amounts of stress in his life. Something is definitely off when all of a sudden, everything he was doing seemed to result in injury to himself or someone else. It was just very unusual for him. Pair that with his abuse of alcohol, steroid use, excessive red meat consumption, and you have someone who had no clue what was really going on in his body. He didn't find out something was wrong with him until it was too late. Once he found out he had kidney failure, his body was already deteriorating so fast he immediately had to start dialysis followed by a series of correlating surgeries. The stress you put on yourself will undoubtedly impact your overall health, and men need to become more aware of this; especially young men who can still make changes before too much damage is done. My friend was just 27 years old when all this happened to him.

My current understanding of food and how it impacts our health shows me how a lifetime of fast foods and processed foods can bring early onset of America's now common lifestyle diseases. Some will blame it on genetics; others will say everything happens for a reason, but I say when it comes to your health, you must learn what signals your body is sending when something is wrong and get help as soon as you can. If you don't know what signals your body is sending you, then how will you know before it's too late?

HOW YOU EAT DETERMINES YOUR LIFESTYLE

If you go out into the dating world and attempt to go out on dinner dates with women, you're certainly going to want to go somewhere where you both can enjoy good food. If she orders a vegetarian dish and you order steak, then it's clear there are some differences in dietary practices that would be sure to make a good conversation point. What you eat and how you consume it will tell a lot about your lifestyle as well as your family's lifestyle. Without a woman who cooks, most men are restaurant and fast food dependent when it comes to food. But it doesn't really matter how nice the restaurant is, most of them serve food with little to no nutrition in it. What you're paying for are convenience and presentation. In all the convenience of fast foods, the quality of the food you eat will always come back to be a major factor in your overall health.

Men scoff at me when I say definitively that it's a man's role to be able to grow and find food for himself and his family. But most men today couldn't grow a blade of grass nor do they know where to find real food outside of the supermarket. That's a far cry from what a man was capable of doing just two generations ago. Men were expected to know how to take to the land and produce food—whether it was for his family's consumption or growing food to be sold. We also had the knowledge of medicinal healing with plants and herbs within our surroundings. We knew where to set up camp and how far water was; we knew our place in nature. Farming or food production might seem like skills and talents are far removed from today's workforce, but it's still necessary in a world where climate change or natural disasters can easily cause food shortages.

Today's women don't choose men based on their ability to grow food nor for their ability to protect them. Women once desired a man who they feel protected by, but a growing proportion of today's women view masculinity in its raw and unpolished state as a threat to their safety. They're being conditioned to welcome a man who is less masculine and feminine in behavior. This way he's viewed universally being of no threat to respond instinctually. Unless he's a construction worker or someone who legitimately works outside with his hands or tools, most women find themselves with gray collar men. Gray collar is a mixture between blue and white collar, but no real tangible skill sets that are geared towards surviving in nature.

The average man reading this book goes to the grocery store for food. That grocery store is likely no more than three-five miles away from his house. His lifestyle is determined by his ability to eat food he can purchase from grocery stores and restaurants. If he were to ever be forced to find food elsewhere, he'd have no clue where to start looking. Pandemonium would ensue. Are you him?

It doesn't have to be if you choose to be smart about your food and your lifestyle. While there's a lot you can't do, growing food might be one of them that you can put yourself in a position to do. If you can't, the next best thing is to purchase and support locally grown foods. If you look around, you'll find farmers and growers growing food somewhere close by you. They may not have everything you're used to getting from the grocery stores, but fresh food is healthier for you. The healthy man must know how to eat well, and his ability to do so will also depend heavily on the women in his life who help with the preparation of the food he eats.

CREATE A HEALTHY ROUTINE

When I changed the way I viewed healthy, it was self-discipline that got me through. I was 20 years old, and in just two years I had gained over 35 pounds from the Standard American Diet lifestyle. I was overweight, but at the time my most pressing health concern was that I was snoring. Instead of trying to lose weight, I was on a quest to stop snoring. But my quest to stop snoring lead me down a road where I eliminated wheat/bread, salt, meat, eggs, and dairy in one giant swoop.

It felt like almost instantly I stopped snoring, but I also lost a total of 50 pounds in 90 days on this program. I actually wasn't in it to lose weight, but I couldn't complain about losing it. I took specific whole food supplements three times daily and avoided all the foods on the do not eat list. I had a busy lifestyle between work and school at that time, but I was able to make time for three dosages of my supplements per day and a willingness to cook every day. I never once felt weak, perhaps because of the supplements. But I was confused about whether the new foods I was eating would be good enough to keep me healthy. Because before this change I was accustomed to eating meat every day. I would never return to eating eggs, and I've never drunk cow's milk since then; however, I did go back to eating bread and cheese. I'd also eat poultry two-three times per month until I stopped eating meat altogether.

It would take me two and a half years to really learn more about a plant-based lifestyle and make a decision to live like that. I wasn't eating much meat and eventually dropped all meats and anything made from an animal. It's now been 12 years living like this, and I'm still learning and evolving because science says one thing, but based on the food we eat today, we clearly don't know as much as we think we know about how food affects our physical and mental health. Healthy will need to be redefined, and what you feed yourself in the sense of thoughts and actions will play a major role in your overall health index.

If taking care of yourself is new to you, then I'm going to help you implement an effective system to help you learn and maintain new habits. I believe the best changes are the smallest changes that you make step-by-step. Step-by-step doesn't have to take you a year. You can completely transform your health and lifestyle within as little as 90-120 days if you're serious. Then you can spend the rest of your life maintaining that same level of health and improving upon it. The determination to make it to another level in your evolution as a man will at some point drive you to make critical changes to your lifestyle. After you make changes, consistency will be the ingredient that carries you the furthest. To assist you on this path, I have here a suggested morning routine based on one of my previous routines. You must know yourself and customize your morning routine to you, but this one can help you as you begin.

MORNING ROUTINE

You need to create an environment where you wake up every day to peace and happiness. This is why being on a break is important—there's no woman who wakes up with you, and it's only your energy present before you. What the morning routine represents more than anything else is your desire to heal yourself and be one with nature; it's a thankful energy that you use to accomplish the objectives of the day. So much beauty happens every morning in nature that we miss out on in our grand rush to the job plantations. The morning routine works best when your mornings are freed up from distractions, and there is no need to be in a rush.

MORNING ROUTINE:

1. *Upon Waking*- Drink as much room temperature natural spring water as you can drink; a liter is great. Breathe deeply. Smile big (even if you don't want to). Face the direction of the sun and embrace thankfulness and the positive possibilities of the day ahead of you.

2. *Affirmations*- Create your first thoughts and make them be positive, self-assuring and absolute. Affirmations are needed self-talk. They can't be based on your ego; they can't be based on or around material objects. They must encourage your spirit. Create affirmations that assure you of your divinity, your talents, and your purpose. Create an unbreakable mindset.

3. *Take your medicine & prepare*- Warm spring water with a squeeze of lime or lemon is good medicine for the colon and the liver. Learn to include herbal teas and extracts into your morning routine.

Find herbs that help you in your growth. Take supplements that you find speak to your body. Prepare something that you eat after you've completed your entire routine; something that helps to energize you without the need for heavy digestion

4. *Get physical-* My preferred morning fitness routine involves a variety of breathing exercises, stretching and calisthenics. It's my own self-taught yoga routine that I like very much. The goal is to perform your movements with grace while building strength and endurance to expand it from just mornings to *multiple times per day.* The body's need to be physical is an important need to be met daily.

5. *Meditate-* If you're able to find meditation within your fitness routine then that would be to your advantage. If not, strive for moments in thoughtlessness where you focus all your thoughts on breathing in and out. You may need to turn all your devices off so you can get this uninterrupted time. Build up your time in meditation minute by minute.

COMMIT YOURSELF & REMIND YOURSELF CONSISTENTLY

1. The morning is the most ideal time to create new habits, especially if you have to be up early most mornings anyways. For mornings to work most effectively, bedtime needs to be in the 10 pm range.

2. It's going to take some time if you're changing for the first time around. But the goal is to make a good transition by adding high-quality foods to your diet along with exercise and positive thinking. Positive thinking with the use of affirmations will help you set your mind up for success.

3. Your goal is to become so disciplined in your morning routine that you can expand the routine to three times per day. Once your morning routine has been perfected, replicating it throughout the day will be an easier process to do. When you seek to do this is when your desire to challenge yourself grows. Be patient with yourself.

A morning routine can help you grab your day before your day grabs you. The skill set it takes to set your mindset for the day and accomplish your daily objectives will drive you to master your days. The morning routine can change your habits, and your lifestyle if you adhere to it. It requires you to disconnect from the typical morning where you're up racing against time to get out of the house. No peace is involved in that. From the moment you wake, you're in a rush most likely to go to work for someone who doesn't share the same ideals as you. As hard as it is to do, some men will have to teach themselves to get up earlier to avoid rushing through the morning.

What I can give you is something like a cheat sheet when it comes to healthy living and eating. A lot of people bite off more than they can chew by doing too much too soon. It doesn't make sense to overload yourself on this process because it can sometimes be slow while at other times a change in what you eat will literally change your entire state of being. You need to know what food and food products you can find naturally occurring vitamins and minerals in. Once you've thrown out the old stuff with chemical additives like yellow #6 and red #40, then you restock with natural food items that are clean. Thereafter, it's about establishing a routine to help you use these newer and healthier foods to your advantage.

FOOLPROOF WHOLE FOOD SUPPLEMENTS

Cayenne pepper

A powerhouse medicinal herb, many people don't take advantage of its healing properties. Cayenne is good for the heart and the veins. It helps strengthen veins and is also an astringent herb that cleanses the body of mucus. It can be taken as powder in water or as capsules. Taking cayenne in the morning will also help to reduce your appetite. Work your way to taking it three times a day, and you'll see how stronger your heart and circulation become. Cayenne is also an effective herb used to subdue bleeding. It has several uses and nothing but benefits to your health.

Blackstrap Molasses

Often forgotten is the sweetness of molasses. Growing up, I hated when my mother would use molasses as a sweetener. Blackstrap molasses is pretty much the only remaining nutrition from the sugar cane process, and if the soil where it comes from is healthy, you'll get essential and trace minerals like copper, selenium, phosphorous, iron and potassium from blackstrap molasses. As strong as it is to swallow, I just take it one tablespoon at a time. I prefer not to mix it in water.

Wheat germ oil

Wheat germ doesn't get much play these days because of other popular oils like hemp seed oil, flaxseed oil, and coconut oil. Wheat germ oil is very nutty oil made from the center seed of the wheat kernel. The oil is rich in vitamins A, B, D and E, and is high in antioxidants. Also a rich source of manganese and copper, wheat germ oil is very rich in uses. It's especially high content of vitamin E makes wheat germ oil an excellent oil for skin care. It is excellent to help prevent scarring.

Apple cider vinegar

Apple cider vinegar is perhaps a universal staple in the kitchen of any cook. It's used for a host of different uses like as dressing on salads; as a vegetable wash for your veggies; in water as a way to help accelerate weight loss or as an astringent to clean your skin and scalp. It's a power food product that has multiple uses and definitely should be kept in the cabinets of your kitchen.

Kelp

In America, women seem to suffer more of the effects of an undernourished thyroid gland, and one of their best friends is kelp. Kelp itself, in its whole state is rich in a variety of sea-based trace minerals, including the one most critical to the thyroid—iodine. These days you have to be cautious as many powdered products are mixed with flour to add body. Kelp is critical to the body's overall performance and helps to regulate the metabolism and the body's natural weight.

LEARN TO EAT AND USE DAILY

- *Fresh leafy greens & veggies-* Find these locally so that way you're not eating overpriced ten-day old kale. If you can get them fresh, eat them within the first two days. To get them fresh, you'll need to grow them yourself or get them from local growers. Find local growers! They'll save your life.

- *Fresh fruits-* Store bought fruits aren't fresh. So do your absolute best to get local fruits. You can't compare a mango coming from Guatemala to one that came from somebody's backyard or farm. In store fruits can be six to 12 months old as is the case for many store bought oranges and apples.

- *Seeds-* Seeds are nutritional powerhouses. Get familiar with adding the likes of hemp, chia, pumpkin, sunflower, almonds, cashews, sesame seeds and others to smoothies and salads. Instant fiber and instant protein. Great source of fat.

- *Juices-* If the only juice you can get is store bought, I understand. But you should want to get to the level where you're juicing your leafy greens at home to extract high-value nutrients that go into the bloodstream superfast. Understand that juices are concentrates that are generally 10x sweeter than just the fruit or vegetable itself. You must not overdo juices. Don't hesitate to dilute with spring water when too sweet.

- *Supplements-* The supplement industry has its bright spots, but for many years people were being sold bottles with labels on them that didn't reflect the actual contents. Men tend to be attracted to dietary supplements that promise to build muscle fast but are filled with synthetics and growth hormones. Look for supplements free of GMOs, soy, gluten and in some cases it might also be good to stay away from ones with grains, too. Trust me; it doesn't have to be a complicated routine if you eat fresh veggies daily.

STAY IN TOUCH WITH YOUR BODY

Men need to start approaching their health in a more holistic manner. This approach to your overall health will help you make the best decisions that not only benefit your personal health, but also the health of the planet. We all must become experts at monitoring our eating, breathing, physical fitness, our elimination, digestions and our stress levels to know our current state of health. We can't be afraid to go to the doctor, but neither can we be afraid to make permanent changes for the better. Maybe all you need is some herbs that are natural and cause no side effects on your body. Maybe you need more. There are basics to healing yourself. If you've lived a life where you grew up on fast food and junk food, it's a great idea to look into long-term cleansing. Don't think that you're going to change 20 or 30 plus years of eating by doing a 21-day juice cleanse. Any cleanse that you do your body will help you rid it of toxins, but eating fresh fruits and vegetables has a long-term cleansing effect as well. We must desire to be masters of our bodies; in tune with all of our frequencies.

KEY BODILY FUNCTIONS MEN MUST BE IN TOUCH WITH TO MONITOR THEIR HEALTH:

1. *Skin, Nails & Hair-* Your skin is your largest organ, and it's constantly detoxifying from the inside out. Some free-floating toxins only get removed from the body when the body is in action, the heart rate increases and you sweat. This is a vital form of detoxifying that we must experience at least three times per week. You must also pay attention to your skin tone, your ability to heal from cuts and wounds, dry skin, itchy skin, skin discoloration, dandruff, balding, eczema, body odor, bad breath, dry scalp, weak fingernails and more. All these things mean something so pay attention.

2. *Prostate-* I say you should eat a prostate friendly diet. And that means ditching the meat, especially red meat. No meat and you get a chance at a strong prostate capable of sex into old age. The trace mineral, selenium is also a good prostate cancer inhibitor. The

essential mineral zinc is also critical to prostate health. Eat foods that are naturally rich in both like pumpkin seeds and Brazil nuts. Seeds are super nutritious and can be mixed into smoothies or sprinkled on top of salads.

3. *Digestion*- Good digestion is becoming a rare thing for most people because our diets include foods that are mostly dead and contain no enzymes nor natural bacteria. We also eat large amounts of proteins that penetrate and damage the intestinal cell walls because we don't quite yet understand how important our guts are to our overall health. These breaches in the intestinal walls weaken the immune system tremendously over a lifetime. This is why at least 90% of all diseases can be eliminated through the eating of healing foods with beneficial enzymes and bacteria. Change the climate in your digestive system by eating more living foods like sauerkraut, kimchi, and pickled foods. All of these foods are better if you made them fresh and raw, but if you purchase them, look for minimally processed versions that are "raw." Adding a strong probiotic to your diet will help get your gut back in action. Connect with me on Facebook or email for recommended brands you can trust.

4. *Elimination*- Elimination must match intake. It would be ideal to go shortly after your meals. Understand that your body collects a lot more that needs to be eliminated than just what you eat. The average body is also ridding itself from waste from all directions—bowels, skin, mucus, urine, etc. It's important to be regular and fiber is a critical part of stimulating elimination. You'll get plenty of fiber from fresh fruits and vegetables, it's just a matter of eating them. You should also get familiar with herbs and foods that are good for helping you eliminate. This is good wisdom to have, too as a new father.

5. *Pancreas*- The principal reason why people end up with a dysfunctional pancreas is overeating. Because the pancreas plays a critical role in digestion, places a lot of pressure on the pancreas to digest frequently. Your pancreas regulates insulin, so the nicer you are to your pancreas, the lower your chances of diabetes are. Your

pancreas is also a hormone regulator; if it's broken or damaged, various hormones will be off, and you will feel it throughout your being. Generally speaking, men aren't often concerned about what's going on the inside, but we must learn to eat foods that feed our internal organs the nutrition they need.

6. *Ejaculation-* Limit them as you get older. Your goal should be one per week if you're active and healthy. As you approach your 50's, you want to do that once per month. You're literally losing essential minerals that are critical to your life force. A man will appear feeble after a lifetime of ejaculating every day. One ejaculation is equivalent to the loss of one pint of blood. Learn to have sex without ejaculating. You'll be in better control, she'll be happier about lovemaking lasting longer and effectively become your own birth control pill.

7. *Strength & Conditioning-* The human body is designed to be in movement upwards of 98% of the time that we're awake. The lifestyle the average man leads in America doesn't involve much movement except for certain manual labor industries. But even these men get used to the labor that comes with the job. Challenging the body to develop through strenuous exercise not only helps to build new muscle, but it also aids in testosterone and hormone regulation as well as increases neurological strengthening in the brain.

My ideal lifestyle is one where everything I do has little to no negative impact on my health and the planet. I believe we need to make our primary objectives to safeguard our health and the health of our physical environment. It's hard to do that when you're already locked into a destructive food system with weak environment policies to protect the earth's natural resources. Most men don't see that what they eat is a major catalyst for not only their health but the health of the planet. The real issue is the fact that most men are oblivious to the actual specifics of their health and the planet. People blindly support the demise of the entire planet by continuing to live a lifestyle that destroys resources to make goods and profit, people included.

Taking care of yourself; mind, body, and soul need to be something men begin to value. You need to become aware of everything that you put on and into your body; the quality of the air you breathe, water you drink and food you eat. You've got to read food product labels and make every effort to eat real food. No matter who provides you with your rations of food, remember that it can never be as fresh or as good for you as the food you grow yourself or that has been locally grown. Your life is happier when your body is feeling healthier. Healthy and happy should go hand in hand because we all should be happy to have the opportunity to create in life.

SEXUAL HEALTH

There are few things as valuable to a man as his ability to have sex. You would think men would do almost anything to maintain good sexual health. But men are largely clueless about what it takes to maintain good sexual potency. Most of us are overstimulated from too much sex or too much exposure to sexual content. What you eat has a lot to do with your sexual potential, and the doctors aren't telling men this information at their checkups. They're either being told that borderline bad health is good enough or are being urged to take prescription drugs that hide problems rather than fix them. Every prescription drug that you take eventually adds to the erosion of your sexual and overall health. To be able to perform at a moment's notice is the epitome of being sexually healthy.

The prostate is important to your sex life, and what you eat affects the longevity of the prostate. The more meat you eat, the higher your risk for prostate cancer is. Prostate health and overall sexual health require a steady supply of zinc in the diet. The prostate responds to zinc dosages. When there is a deficiency, the prostate will swell and begin to become tight and uncomfortable. Zinc helps to maximize testosterone production and also helps to store existing testosterone reserves.

The trace mineral selenium is also another important nutrient to help maintain a healthy prostate. Selenium not only reduces your chances of cancer, but it's been shown that when combined with adequate amounts of vitamin E, selenium increases sperm mobility and quality. It's a matter of understanding how to eat to nourish your prostate. The more bad foods you avoid, the healthier the entire system is.

High cholesterol levels will also impact sexual health. The heavy meat consumption that contributes to high cholesterol levels also leads to poor blood circulation throughout the entire body. So while it may work when you get it up, poor circulation can have you in a position where it may not come alive when you need it to. If you're a man who's under 40, please believe you're not exempt if you don't take care of yourself. Every year, younger and younger men are suffering from health complications such as high blood pressure and high cholesterol, lifestyle diseases that were once typically expected of men closer to the age of 50.

HEALTHY SEX

Sex is magic, but it's not just physical magic. It's spiritual magic and healing magic, too. You can either view your sex drive as one that drives you to reproduce or one that connects you to a woman. Healthy sex can only happen between healthy people. There's so much more than fluids being exchanged during sexual intercourse. Bodily fluids certainly dominate the physical aspect, but how we connect is so much deeper.

Whether you are upfront about it or not, your thoughts and your energy are being shared with her. We impart much more than our DNA into the women we have intercourse with. We also impart our dreams, our fears, our happiness and our sadness. It's important to understand that there's a merging going on when you're intimate with her, and your thoughts at that moment are important because she will feel it. Negative thoughts about yourself or negative thoughts about sex can lead you to impart negativity onto her, and many men must know they have that power. It's so important for sex to be sacred in a time where it has lost its value and role. We are hurt people having hurt sex, and we are all collectively sharing our pain with each other. Sex provides you the opportunity to empower your partner physically and emotionally. When a man penetrates a woman with the intentions of healing her, loving her and protecting her, she will feel it, and if she's not healthy enough to accept it, she will reject it in some form. She might be happy with the sex, but if she cannot receive your energy through sexual transmutation, then she'll seek to receive that energy elsewhere, through other means. Never be distraught by the woman who cannot receive your energy. Not every woman is a perfect fit. And there are times where you can be enjoying the sex and giving what you consider to be the best to someone who takes it with no intention of reciprocating the effort. Hurts, but we're all hurt people in some fashion.

Many men have been broken by unhealthy sex. Unhealthy sex is not only pertaining to diseases of the body but also disease of the mind and the spirit. Sex is strong medicine, and we live in a culture where more and more young women have been sexually assaulted by men, sometimes their very own family members. This is the disease of self-hate that's being injected into our young women. And with the increase in perversion, our young boys are also being injected with this form of sexual repression that leads to sexual misconduct and crimes. Sexual health is important on so many other levels besides being able to perform. Men, we have the power to light a woman up like a Christmas tree if our energy is strong enough. If you take care of your overall health and your sexual organs, you will be able to use sex to heal yourself and your partner, rather than as tool to oppress or abuse. Good sex should be one of our most transformative tools in helping unite man and woman again for the purpose of building stronger families and communities.

SEX DRIVE BOOSTING FOODS

So just like there are foods you eat that lower your sex drive, there are foods you can eat that will give it a boost. The foods that are going to lower your sexual potency are the typical foods you should be avoiding anyways—bacon and bacon anything, steaks and red meat and cholesterol loaded shrimp and shellfish. There are more poisons like prescription drugs, but let's keep it basic and understand that all of these foods are designed to lower your vibration.

Eating foods that are good for your sex drive is easy because they're foods you're already familiar with, but you may not have known that they can keep you alert like a guard dog.

Avocados

Known to the ancient Aztecs as the "testicle tree," avocados are rich in folate. Folate is a very important component to sperm strength and mobility. Research has estimated that men with low levels of folate may have as much as 20% less healthy sperm.

How to eat: guacamole dip, cut avocado on salads and sandwiches

Watermelon

Fruits of the vine have been revered as sexual stimulants since ancient times. Watermelon, the ever-popular summertime fruit has in its flesh and into the rind/skin the amino acid citrulline– whose beneficial functions are now being discovered. Among them is the ability to relax blood vessels, much like Viagra does to the body. The relaxed blood vessels can lead to increased blood circulation to those special regions.

How to eat: Eat it whole, all by yourself if you may. Eat into the rind—that's where a lot of the Viagra-like properties are.

Bananas

Bananas are high in the enzyme bromelain and b vitamins, both of which have been shown to be potent sexual hormone regulators that can increase sexual desire, sexual function, and overall virility. Bananas are also filled with potassium which produces sex hormones and magnesium which aids in producing sex hormones such as androgen, estrogen, and neurotransmitters that regulate the sex drive—such as dopamine and epinephrine.

How to eat: Bananas are perfect in a variety of combinations. They go well with almost every other fruit. Eat plain or freeze and add to your daily smoothies.

Maca

A staple in the high mountainous regions of Peru, Maca is treasured among locals who survive on it and is now widely available in powder form. There are red, black and yellow maca, and they vary with their effects on the body. Black maca has been shown to have positive effects on sperm production, more than yellow maca and red maca. Red maca has been shown to reduce prostate size in studies done on male rats.

How to eat: Maca powders can easily be added to your smoothies as well as added to non-dairy milk

Pumpkin seeds

Just to show you how late most of us are, pumpkin seeds were used in the early 1900s to treat symptoms of enlarged prostates and other symptoms of urinary tract problems. Pumpkin seeds are high in zinc and an excellent natural form of this essential mineral. Pumpkin seeds also contain high levels of vitamins E, C, D, K and B as well as many of the essential sex drive minerals such as potassium, calcium, niacin and phosphorous.

Zinc is paramount to the entire reproductive system. It's estimated that as much as 40% of adult males are zinc deficient. Zinc is a primary mineral required by the prostate, used in sperm production and shown to reduce prostate diseases. Zinc deficiency has been linked to low testosterone levels in men (1), enlarged prostate, balding and even prostate cancer.

How to eat: Add pumpkin seeds to salads as a topping; add them to your smoothies or add them to baked dishes like banana bread. Roast raw seeds for an additional kick.

Reference:
http://www.ncbi.nlm.nih.gov/pubmed/8875519

SEXUAL KUNG FU

If you're going to be taking all these precautions to protect your sexual health, then you're going to want to have some skills to go with all this sexual health you've got. When you're eating an optimum diet, your sexual potency will have the greatest opportunity to grow, but only if you take the time to work on this area. Some men think it's all about sticking their penis into a woman's vagina and going in and out until he ejaculates. Sometimes it's that simple, but as you get older, it becomes more than just gyrating to ejaculate.

Becoming a better lover will require the strengthening and conditioning of your entire sexual reproductive organs. Many men should consider full body detoxes and cleanses that help you rejuvenate your sexual organs. This will give you the unique opportunity to fully excel in the sacred art of lovemaking. Ultimately, it's the passionate love maker capable of fully satisfying a woman's sexual needs who holds a special place in her heart. Pair that with your ability to make her feel secure, and she should be your number one supporter. The world has changed our role identifications with each other, women yearn for things that solidify their security in this material world, but their need for sexual fulfillment is and will always be a driving force behind their desires for a man and a family. Any improvements you make in this department will serve you well. You'd like to be that unexpected bombastic, fantastic, romantic lover! But usually, women can tell beforehand.

It will be important to understand your male anatomy and learn how you can master it for better sexual mastery. Ejaculation control will become very important to a man as he ages. If his health is compromised, ejaculation control needs to be used immediately. A unique way to look at it is that with ejaculation control, you get to be your own birth control pill. You get to extend lovemaking for as long as it takes to transmute sexual energy with her into healing bliss.

Consider your penis and entire genital region just like your arms and your legs that can benefit from exercise. You don't want to overwork it without doing things that can strengthen the region and help increase the potency of it.

Easy exercises you can learn right now:

1. Buttocks Grips- Your glutinous maximus muscle is responsible for upwards of 90% of your thrusting strength. When your muscles are conditioned, each deep thrust is electric like a light saber.
   - Stand with feet a shoulder's width apart
   - Squeeze buttocks together as tightly as you can
   - Hold for 15 seconds and release
   - Warm up with 3-5 sets to feel a burn
   - Lay flat on the floor with hands to the side and squeeze for 45 seconds
   - Release and squeeze buttocks rapidly, nonstop until you can't anymore
   - Rest for 30 seconds
   - Repeat 5 more sets
   - Rest one minute
   - Squeeze and hold buttocks for 60 seconds
   - No rest, rapidly squeeze buttocks for 60 seconds
   - Complete four sets of these '

2. Urine Stop Exercise
   - With full bladder, contract your PC muscle
   - Hold for three seconds & release
   - Raise up and down your heels three-five times each urination
   - Gradually increase hold time
   - This exercise strengthens all the body tendons and sexual energy parts

3. Eye rolling & breathing during sex
   - Circulate eyes clockwise
   - Circulate eyes counter clockwise
   - Visualize your breath and pull your ejaculation up when you inhale
   - Disperse the energy when you exhale to all of your body parts
   - Your breath controls your heartbeat as well as your ejaculation
   - Lose control of your breath and you lose your life force via ejaculation

The typical American male doesn't value his health on the level that he should. We're encouraged to eat harmful foods that degenerate our bodies and we top that off with excessive amounts of sex and ejaculation. We weren't taught how valuable those fluids are to a man's overall health. Many men are oversexed from early in their teenage years and spend decades chasing after women and sex without knowing that they've become sex addicts. One ejaculation is equivalent to the loss of a pint of blood, according to the teachings of Taoist sexual energy practices. This is why there are levels to sex. Some people are in too bad of a shape to be coming every night because for men who aren't happy with where they are in life nor happy with their sexual performance will fall easily into depression with excessive ejaculations. At first it might seem like a stress reliever, but then it becomes your Achilles heel. It can control you.

These exercises I highlight are all simple to do and only the eye rolling and breathing during sex exercise needs a partner. Other than that, on a good relationship break you can find time to get your practice on. Nothing beats solo masturbation with a withdrawal instead of ejaculation. This is the easiest way to build skills. Feeling it coming and stop. Then eventually you can feel it coming while continuing to stimulate yourself and voluntarily dissipate your orgasm energy while continuing to make love. If you take a break to be celibate, but your sex drive is still turned up, this kind of solo practice will prove to be very beneficial to your future sex life. When it's time for sex again you won't be worried about if you're going to come too fast. These techniques develop strength where you need it, because after all, it is a muscle. One you can train to perform for you. But also a valuable tool in your arsenal as you take care of yourself to the highest degree. A confident lover with purpose is a force to be reckoned with.

BACK ON THE MARKET
AFTER A BREAK

DATING WOMEN SHOULD BE A different experience after your break because it becomes something you do consciously rather than casually.

Understand that many women are accustomed to suckers who either have no clue on how to treat a woman and are still recovering from their childhood challengers- mommy issues, missing fathers, self-esteem issues and/or rough neighborhoods where incarceration rates are extremely high. Many women have had their hearts broken by men from these conditions, so they recognize this these men immediately, yet still they can't resist his pull. Unfortunately, many women have gotten so accustomed to these kind of men that they don't know how to respond to a man who not only brings substance to the table but is interested in taking the time to get to know who she really is. As a man, you increase your value tremendously when you're actually trying to get to know her without the expectation of sexual intimacy. She decreases her value when, unfortunately for her, she's not accustomed to answering real questions and has a hard time opening up about herself. As beautiful as she may be, the men she's accustomed to are surface level and while she may have been with a few of them intimately, she's never revealed her vulnerability to any of them. Many women today prefer a man who doesn't dig deeper than the surface; someone who is more concerned about their physical appearance rather than their mental and spiritual state of being. With this guy all she has to do is look good and go along with his sexual demands and she's accepted. Many women, just like the men they encounter, don't know what they want out of a partner and will settle for the status quo relationship if it looks and feels good in the moment.

That's why when you start dating again you have to change your entire approach to women. After your break, you now value your time. You won't waste your time chasing women when you could be working on accomplishing our life's mission.

SELF-VALUE AFTER YOUR BREAK

This chapter is a handbook on how to reemerge into the dating world feeling like you hit the self-lottery twice. After a good break, you will feel the immense amount of value that you've added to yourself. You're going to want to make sure that whoever you invest time into is, first of all, your type and secondly someone who can understand the needs of an evolving man. But get this, you have less time to figure this out than you've ever had before. There's a new premium on your time; you can't waste your time or throw it in the direction of women based on their ease of availability. You're just going to have to get used saying no to women who in the past you'd have fucked.

Ironically, women love to hear about your break from sex and relationships. They tend to want to hear what was that like for you, why'd you do it, what did you learn and what's going to be so different moving forward. Even though they may not have known you previously, they want you to be a better version of yourself for your benefit and also if there's a chance they may end up with you. Women love to hear about your growth, so be sincere about your process when you speak about it. But be careful of how much time you spend talking about yourself in the beginning. If she's really interested in you, she'll ask you specific questions, and you'll notice she takes a lot of initiative to get to know more about you. Women want an elevator speech or a dashing introduction of who you are, where you're from, what you do and why her life would be better if she fell in love with you. Men of distinction do a very good job of communicating their value to women without touting their credentials. They also can effortlessly communicate a vision of things to come to women.

A good sign to pay attention to is when she takes early interest in your vision for your life. You paint the picture of the life you want to lead and let her envision herself being your woman. You won't have to talk much about yourself, if she's interested in you she'll talk to you or no one else. You won't have to convince her to wait for you if you two can't be together right now, she will wait if she has chosen you and you chose her, too. All you'll have to do is take your time getting to know if she's an ideal fit for the life you want to lead. If she is, then take your time to get acquainted with her, her family and her lifestyle. If she's an American woman, the more time you spend getting to know her, the better your chances will be at success. American influenced women are often confused in regards to what level of commitment or submissiveness they are willing to give to a man. They've been heavily influenced to remain guarded and independent, never showing their vulnerability for the fear of being used for sex.

What high value men don't do is jump in bed with unqualified women who may either get pregnant or hang around in your life for the purpose causing distractions to your work. If you move too fast too soon, then you're setting yourself up for failure; especially with an American woman. Over stimulation of the sexual glands will lead to a weakened willpower that will find every excuse to blow off some steam rather than to continue working until there's a breakthrough. What a man on a mission knows is that he cannot afford the setbacks of being distracted by early attraction to women. When the time has come where spending time getting to know a woman isn't a distraction from getting your work done, then you can enjoy the process more without as many restraints. Until you have that free reign, you must sparingly spend your time dating.

NO PREMATURE SEX

Every new relationship should have an extended period of observation where you take time to get to know who a woman truly is. This can be the way you show her that you actually value yourself. What you're

saying is that you're not going to sign a contract with her before you
know everything about what you'd be signing up for. You're supposed
to enjoy the process; go out and meet women who are more likely to be
your type. Get conversational and let them know you want to hang out
with them again. Do all this, but don't change your routine and don't
make yourself more available to date one or multiple women. Always
seek to maximize the return you can get from pursuing your dream life
first. Be loyal and devotional to your purpose and never give it a back
seat to dating. If you don't get to talk to her but once or twice per week
in the beginning, that's fine. She's lucky it's not once every two weeks.

You've got to be wise enough to understand that having sex too
soon can ruin your underdeveloped reputation with her, even if she
willingly gives it up. Neediness for sex is often an indicator that you
didn't do enough self-work on your break, and you're in need of the
validation that comes with sex. Or you're still overstimulated like many
men are. You shouldn't come out of your break feeling desperate for
the company of women or sex. If your need for sex and the company
of women is what is driving you to date again then you should go back
on a break to do more self-reflection and sexual desensitization. If this
is ever the case, your overstimulated sex drive is preventing you from
dealing with the true void that you have so it seeks to fill that gap with
the familiar pleasure of sex, or perhaps masturbation.

When a man is truly on the market to find a wife-caliber woman
to settle down with, some women will be able to pick up on high
sexual energy and position themselves for the short term to give you
what you're too weak to resist as well as reap some of the benefits that
you'll extend unto her. Even if she knows she's not your long-term
match, some women have mystical powers over you when they make
love to you that make you temporarily feel like she's the one even if
you know she's not. That's why you must be strong enough to resist
the temptation of having sex altogether. After a break where you've
been without sex for a while, your body might be screaming out to be
touched by the opposite sex, but you must protect yourself from too

much too soon. It can be overload on your sensory factors if you move too fast in the direction of sex and commitment. Most things that start fast end fast, too.

A truly restorative break will shake you up so much that you will literally think twice every time a situation arises where sex is a potential outcome with a woman you don't know very well. You'll think thoughts like—what does it say about me if I allow us to have sex? Or what if she catches feelings and wants to get serious before I'm ready? Is this someone I want to be connected to? These are legitimate questions that once upon a time most men were told to ignore. But you shouldn't have sex with her if you don't have concrete answers to those questions. If a woman feels you're what she wants, in the beginning she'll sign up for whatever you sign up for to get your commitment to her. If you're having sex before at least seven dates, then you still don't know jack shit about her yet. And I already told you, I feel one date every 10-14 days in the beginning is a good starting pace for man whose purpose is his first priority.

You couldn't know her very well if you're having sex before you met her father and her family or before she's met any of your friends and family. This would just be sex with a beautiful and hopeful stranger. Sometimes it makes for good times, but it rarely ever turns into anything beneficial to a man. Men break these rules all the time, and while some make it out safely, many men don't. Men think they're the ones who have been working the magic to get her to open her legs and keep them open when all along it's a seductive woman working her voodoo on you. If she got you in bed before you fully explored all of your options with other strong candidates like her, you're going to be mad at yourself because sleeping with her could mean you signed a contract to be with her and keep her around. If you end up sleeping with someone new after a few dates, but you're absolutely thrilled about her as a person, you must still tread carefully because even what you see and experience with your own eyes, in the beginning, can be a manipulative illusion. Time will always be the master that reveals to you what you don't see right away. Sex is not the goal. You must lower your need for validation through sexual intimacy and make organic chemistry with interested women to better determine your compatibility. When you're in alignment with your purpose, and you know what you want in life, you just might meet the perfect stranger, find out you two agree, make love and live happily ever after together. It can happen just like that, but it won't happen so easily if you have a lot of baggage and past pain you're still holding on to when you meet new women. Your relationship break is where you get to put down a lot of this baggage through self-reflection, forgiveness, self-love and dedication to your purpose. Your break can be your re birth if you give yourself enough time.

DATING WITHOUT SEX

The best part of dating without sex is that you get the best of both worlds: you get to be single, and you get to enjoy the company of beautiful women. You already know that they can't dominate your time, but it's perfectly ok to think about the one you feel most compatible with while you work diligently towards your purpose. Many men don't have the initial discipline to refuse overt sexual advances from women who want their attention. Being back on the market doesn't mean you bombard yourself with women on your search for the one. Remember, your break was to focus on you. Don't start dating again only to end up taking that focus off you and placing it back on women. That's a no-no that many men quickly fall back into. Dating from this position is about effortlessly communicating your value as a husband and companion, while working tirelessly to accomplish your life's mission before you can spend large amounts of time with her. You never want to endanger or slow your path to success for the opportunity to pursue new relationships. My dad always said that women will always be there and it's taken me years to fully understand what this means. What it means is that whatever you have to offer, you can offer more of it once you've first taken the time to develop it while single. Women will definitely be there once you're more secure in your position in life. Dating without sex is old school.

It's actually the process of befriending a woman that you're perfecting in the early going. Sadly, so many men have grown accustomed to moving so fast that they end up sleeping with women who they have no friendship with. This is even more sad and destructive when a man gets a woman he has no real connection to pregnant. Women reveal their vulnerability to their friends and they're very weary of men who they've put in the friend zone. However, if you put her in the friend zone early for the purposes of getting to know her better, she may be determined to charm you into giving her more time and commitment in exchange for an incentive. The minute you fall for this, you move from the driver's seat to the passenger seat and your potential friendship will be at risk. Men must develop the discipline to say no to women who want you to overcommit to them. The modern woman tends to believe that her power lies within her sexual prowess. You mustn't fall for the feminine charm because after all, it's a test of your strength and your discipline. She wants to know she can't control you, but she will still use her femininity and attractiveness to lure you off track. If you invest in a valuable friendship, you need to be able to see how committed she can be at playing this friendship role. Call on her when you need her and build trust with her when you speak. You've got to be able to keep her interested without spending an exorbitant amount of time doing so. It's always a smart idea for men to also put a few beautiful women who are on your level in the friend zone. They usually hate being just a friend and are relentless in their quest to get you off your plan and into theirs. But this is a good way to exercise discipline and restraint for men who draw a lot of interest from women. They can't all have what they want and you must be willing to communicate to them that they can be so much more to you if they can encourage you to stay committed to your path before you commit to a woman you've been dating.

PREPARE YOURSELF BEFORE YOU GO FOR HER

Take the extra time to do your scouting report on where you're going and the type of women you'll meet there. Don't go to places where your ideal mate wouldn't be. I've met many women in the grocery store because I like to eat, and I like a woman who likes to eat and cook. It's almost an instant connection for me if when I meet a woman who enjoys cooking and eating good food. Find places to go where it's not about the use of pickup lines or approaching a large amount of women to increase your closing ratio. I've never felt I've had an issue with sparking interest with the women I meet, so I'll never be the guy anymore who's just out there practicing pickup lines. I say go straight for the one you like the most, based on all the contributing factors that attracted you to her.

Depending on when you started your family will also determine how hard you work, but how hard you work can also be determined by how smart you work. My belief is that the job of conquering the world is a full time job that requires very little time off in the early stages of that process. Prematurely giving that time to women you just met is not a progressive move for your goals. As long as sex is not your motivator, you can gradually spend more time befriending her, but your work and your life must be manageable. And her friendship, which is like extended courtship, must be valuable and motivating.

Here are some things you want to do with her and know about her in the early stages of your friendship, way before intimacy ever comes up:

1. *Qualify everything.* Take time to get to know her; especially the experiences that she feels have shaped who she is today. This is time you take to find out if she's in possession of the attributes you need in a wife. You also want to make sure you can give her what she wants in love and life.

2. *Have fun.* If you both enjoy each other's company, then fun should be automatic. If she's attracted to you, she'll probably think you're really funny without trying too hard. In the beginning,

refrain from getting too technical in conversation; you don't want her to be overthinking because she'll eventually close up. If you work hard, you deserve fun and conversation with someone both attractive and compatible.

3. *Learn her state of mind.* Higher level conversations must take place before any kind of intimacy does. Her lifestyle will tell you about how she thinks, so pay attention to as much details as you can when you're getting to know her. Before you get invested, you must know how sound her judgment and problem-solving skills are. Is her faith strong? Is she loyal? You shouldn't necessarily ask her a series of complicated questions, but you should be able to know by the position she takes on different stances over time.

4. *Self-disclosure.* You don't have to spill the entire bean pouch, but make sure you voluntarily tell her enough about yourself for her to get a truthful idea of what kind of person you are. Stagger things so she feels there's always something new to learn about you—don't tell her everything all at once, but be willing to if the opportunity presents itself or if she asks. She's going to trust you based on who you say you are and who you show yourself to be. Be mindful if she seems uninterested in disclosing more about herself; that's a major red flag.

5. *Know why she likes you.* Women like me because I'm good looking, intelligent, ambitious and a good cook. They like me for more, but they love me for these things. I'm comfortable about this, and I keep an eye open for other things women may like about me. You want someone who tells you what she likes about you so you're not left guessing why she likes you. If you give enough of yourself, it'll be very clear what she's most attracted to about you.

6. *She chose you.* Mature, high-value women communicate their love intentions verbally and non-verbally. Nobody has time to be guessing if she really wants to be with you. If you like her right away, and you know she likes you back, then everything is Gucci. Just make sure that she's liking you more with time and it's not

fading away as the dates go on. Some women like you this week or this month but are on to their next thrill the next week or next month. No high-value man has time for those kind of women.

SHOWING YOUR FEELINGS FOR HER

The feeling you want to get from every woman that you meet is that, I can't wait to get to school each morning, kind of feeling. When you get that feeling, and she has it, too, it's such a beautiful feeling for you both. If you've taken your time to get to know her and you begin to have feelings for her, this is a sign of progress. This is the point where you must trust yourself to eventually close the deal. All you're required to do from this point out is to continue sharing yourself and this feeling with her. Don't listen to anyone that's selling you tactics. If as much as six months have passed and within that time you've developed a friendship that she is ready to convert into marriage and intimacy, you should trust what you feel. At this stage, you shouldn't have to wonder whether or not she wants to be with you. It will be clear. She also shouldn't have to question her value in your eyes. She should feel loved and she should be bursting with excitement at the idea of being permanently committed to you and the family you two will build together. If you've made it clear where you want the relationship to go, you must guide the courtship in that direction without being distracted by sex, expectations of others or even your own ego's delusional needs. You must lead the relationship in the direction you said you would, but never get too caught up in leading. Mature women have an incredible amount of valuable input that can add value to your position. Leaning on her for her input shows that you value her insight and encourages her to take an active role in your life.

Another key to success in this arena where there's no sex is not to idolize sex. You don't want to hold sex as some kind of prize or reward that you get after a period of time. As crazy as this may sound, you should be willing to wait as long as possible or even until marriage. If you feel that the chemistry is consistently growing each time you talk or spend time together then you two will draw nearer and nearer to each other physically. When chemistry is undeniable, sex becomes harder to avoid, but it creates excitement. The new truth is, if the chemistry is still good after time passes and she's in full support of the man you're evolving into, then propose to her. Get engaged and start making concrete plans for a life together. When you've done all your pre-work, you no longer need to think on the lines of "what if this doesn't work?" You actually stop thinking and allow yourself to feel. Allowing yourself to feel will test your vulnerability and show her your added dimensions.

CONVERSATION STARTERS

When you get back out there from a break, you have new tools in your toolkit to qualify and eliminate women who may just be frauds looking for a nice outing. It's all about conversation at this point. The key is not to get overly analytical in your conversation. You also shouldn't be afraid to end dates with new prospects if you find out she's not what you're looking for. But you must be daring in your ability to create new engaging conversations that reveal valuable insight to each other.

Critical conversation topics:

Current Events

The newspaper era is dead and many people aren't fully aware of what's going on in their world. It may not matter to you if she's totally clueless about what's going on in the world, but it's always good to be able to hold a relevant conversation about the things that are impacting us in our perspective worlds today. Some men want a woman to watch the morning or evening news with.

Social Issues

There's a special connection between two people when they find out that they share the same social interests. Don't be afraid to show how passionate you are bout causes near and dear to your heart. If she ends up feeling the same way as you do about the same cause, then this could be a great way to connect further. You guys could find out you have the same passion for education, religion, politics, entertainment or even food. It's always good if you can find a common ground where you both share an equal amount of interest.

Lightheartedness

When it comes to being out with a woman you like, it's important to keep it fun and light. If she likes you, she'll laugh at your jokes. The key here is to have and create a fun atmosphere that can lead to closeness (not sex). Just don't laugh at your own jokes more than she does. Your jokes should show confidence and that you're not afraid to poke fun at things and even her. During a good laugh would be a nice time to touch her hand or shoulder lightly to see how she responds to your touch. Take it as a good sign if she reaches out and touches you, too.

Marriage

A woman who's serious about marriage will mention her desire to be married while a man who's looking for a wife need only make mention of his credentials that qualify him as good husband material. Saying you're saving to buy a home is just as good as saying I'd like to get married and start a family soon. Find creative ways to talk about marriage without sounding like the guy who just wants to get married. Then hear her out and truly find out what her expectations are; all you need to be is an eligible bachelor who knows his value and what he brings to the table, she'll take it upon herself to indicate to you her willingness to marry you. Insert lighthearted mentions about different components of marriage such as sex, children, and finances to see where she takes the conversation.

Adventure

Women love men who have a strong sense of adventure; men who want to do more than just Netflix and chill. If a woman feels she can gain from your existing adventurousness, then they'll be all ears to hear about all the things you like to do. It's nice when you've lived an adventurous life and can share some of those experiences with her. Be sure to mention the things you like to do, not things that you think she'd like to do. If she likes what you like, then invite her to do it along with you and make sure she has blast with you. You never know, you may play pickup basketball twice per month, and she's a good shooter. Adventures don't have to be all physical or outdoor, sometimes you just gotta make up some wild shit to do on a random day and see if she's down for the ride.

BODY LANGUAGE

You've got to be intuitive when talking to women on dates or on the spot. You have to be able to pick up on the energy she's giving you right away. If she's interested in you, she'll give you a lot of signs that tell you that she's interested. If she's not interested, you're going to have to make sure that she's not just being nice to you. You don't want a sympathy conversation, sympathy telephone number or sympathy smile. It kills me when women do this to men, but are not interested in them at all. If you key in on her body language alone, that will eliminate some of the guesswork for you. Don't waste time on women who don't give you buying signs, and they are all in her body language.

- **Playing with her hair**- This is one of the biggest signs that she's calling for your attention. Ever looked at a woman once, then looked again and she's now playing in her hair? She's calling you! Go get her!
- **Eye contact**- Ever walked by a woman and you both locked eyes? Did you look away and look back again, and she was still staring

at you? Ideally speaking, it's best to approach her once you see that she's looking at you intently. She wants you! Approach her!

- **Direction**- You saw her when you walked in the store, but you were headed in a completely different direction than her, but somehow she's completely facing you now. She wants you to see her so you know not to leave before you approach her. Take that as a sign of interest. Go get her!
- **Closeness**- Is she closer to you than normal in a conversation? Does she lean in to listen to what you have to say? Did she go out of her way to get a little closer to you? Those are all major buying signs. She's interested!
- **Touch**- Women have subtle ways of telling they want you. Did you just meet her, crack a joke and somehow her soft and gentle hand ended up on your arm while she was laughing? Don't overlook that. Close the deal.

FOCUS ON THE APPROACH

Most women complain about men not approaching them often enough because most men have problems approaching women. Sometimes, it can be awkward, but it's like an adventure men must learn how to embrace. The more you do it, the easier it becomes for you. This isn't exactly a book about how to approach women, but you must have the self-confidence needed approach the women you are interested in. I know most of us have had our self-confidence shaken in some shape or form, but your self-confidence increases tremendously after making yourself your number one priority. These are just a few pointers that help me recognize when a woman is interested in me. I had to learn them because I was missing key opportunities to approach women I like because I wasn't reading the right signs. Paying attention to body language has helped me be more confident about my approach because I generally move in when I get tipped off by one or more of the signals.

For some men, your break might need to be focused on building up the courage it takes to approach women who you find attractive. Some guys never had enough practice with their approach and weren't confident enough to go after who they wanted. If that's the case, do the necessary self-work gain the confidence needed to make effective approaches. The more women you can hold valuable conversations with, the more confident you'll become in your approach.

History has shown that it's always made a better storyline when the purpose driven man seeks after his purpose and returns to find a love that is proud of his accomplishments. It just works better like that for some reason. Providing that you take a real break from relationships, you should drench yourself in your work and when you do decide to date, that will speak for you. You just can't lose your swagger in working too much. I've actually been there, and as good as that might be for your career objectives, it's not what makes women excited about you unless she's the "need the security of a stable man type." They exist, and there's nothing wrong with them if they work well with you. There's nothing more attractive to a woman than a man who knows what he wants in life and is dedicated to it. When you hit the scene looking to spark conversation with new women, you are not desperate, you're not needy, you're not clingy, you're not overly sensitive, you don't have your guards up, you're willing to trust, and you feel sure of yourself. You're there to mingle and find a good match for you. You're not looking to jump into bed with the first good looking woman that gives you the green light. You now value yourself enough to know that free and easy sex can cost you time and possibly your peace of mind.

Once you've polished up your conversation skills and know how to take cues from women, you're in the best position to close as many deals as possible. The best options to have are the options you're really excited about- the one's you're most attracted to. If you go out some-where, you want it to be somewhere you're likely to find like-minded women to talk to. You should have a feel for the room and you should always keep your eyes on who you find attractive as well as who is checking you out. I prefer to go places where other friends and associ-ates are also present. That boosts my social status and women who are interested in you will be checking to see if you're well known or if you two share mutual friends.

I try to avoid the nightclub scene because the women there are rarely marriage material. When I do the nightclub scene, it's usually with my comrades and I'm never looking for anyone to take interest in. I'd rather events where there are like-minded women who are easily approachable present. At least if they're at an event about a social issue I care about, then it's a higher probability that it's also something that she cares about. I've been wrong about this, but I've been right more than wrong.

CLOSING THE DEAL

Once your approach can get you in the door with new women, you should be able to qualify and/or eliminate them by the second to third time you speak. If an outing netted you three contacts, within a week you should be down to just one or none. If you're down to one and you like her, make arrangements for your first date within those first three conversations following the first time you met. Make sure you treat your time like the valuable commodity that it is. Don't' accept flaky and uncertain time commitments from women who want to slot you as an option on their dating wheel. You set the time, and if she can't make it, then may you consider her again when you have time again, but probably not. This approach will eliminate women who will not take you seriously, but are looking for guys to add to their fan club. You're not a fan. You're a coach looking for your star player.

To even remotely be interested in marriage, you must feel like you've found a woman who is a rare gem and for most men today, that will not be an easy find. High-value women aren't a dime a dozen. They tend to come along after you've become a high-value man and have been through the fire of becoming your own man. This is what women respect; event he women who rebel against a man who is firm still respects his strong positioning of himself.

Men of distinction marry women who can encourage their growth and love them despite their commitment and dedication to their purpose or calling. Men like this can't marry attention whores. They must marry women of substance who can help bolster their cause in life. Many unsuspecting men have gotten themselves caught up in the looks of a superficial woman without realizing that she's not committed to him or his plans for the future. I'm hoping that this book can help you avoid this fate. Total commitment to your purpose in life will help you choose a woman who fits into your lifestyle. If you can't commit to the time to get to know her beforehand, then you can't get married. That simple. Marriage isn't as necessary when you're young and still in search of your big break. It's loneliness you have to combat in the meantime. Ultimately, if you follow these rules of engagement, starting with how you value yourself and your time, you'll filter out most of the women who are pretenders. The best way to find out who she truly is to be her friend. Do that first and the friendship will tell you all you need to know on whether she's someone who wants to be connected to you for the rest of her life.

A BALANCED APPROACH
TO FAMILY

AROUND THE TIME WHEN I was making some of my biggest mistakes with women was also a time where my soul was yearning for a woman who could be my wife and companion. I hadn't yet recognized the source of this internal calling and certainly didn't know how to express it to anyone at the time. By the time I was around 27, I no longer had a strong drive to be with many women at the same time like I once did. I wanted more. I wanted someone who was compatible with me; someone who I can have a long term love with. Instead, I was expecting a child from woman I hardly knew at a time when I was rediscovering my purpose in life. I believed I was ready to be a father. How hard could it be, I thought.

But I wasn't ready to be a family man quite yet. I perhaps thought I was, but in retrospect, I know I wasn't. I wanted to accomplish a few more things on my own before I felt I was ready to be totally committed to a family unit. Another major reason why I wasn't ready to commit was because I didn't feel as if I found the right partner. Right or wrong for me, she was certainly having our baby. She was beautiful, talented and had great potential, but I could never feel anything she was giving to me at the time so there was no genuine connection. This is a matter of chemistry and compatibility; if she's the one for you, she'll adjust herself accordingly to accommodate your needs. And if she's not the one, neither of you will make the necessary sacrifices to push the relationship further along. It's sad when children are involved and people have to go their separate ways, but the sooner it is clear to all parties that separation is what's best, the sooner you should go your separate ways before your incompatibilities assassinate both your characters.

SHE'S THE ONE

There are many concepts out there in determining who the right woman for you is, but I believe the most telling sign that she's the one is the impact that she has on your life. Your ideal helpmate is an impact player that makes an impact with whatever she brings to the table. She's a team player who sees value in working together with you. This woman is one who knows how to give to you based on your needs, not based on contemporary ideals of what a man wants or needs, but your specific tailor made needs. What she brings to the table could be as simple as encouragement and support for you on your path or good partnering skills that allow you to focus on being a better provider, protector, and leader while she handles the other intangibles. Every woman is different, so every man needs to be in alignment with what his needs are to feel confident that he has chosen the right one for him. As a man, your needs are important. I've done the whole, "she'll come around in due time thing," and I advise against it because people are more likely to remain the same than change. Don't fool yourself into thinking that a woman who isn't loving you the way you want love will eventually love you more when she sees how much you put into the relationship. She's not the one if she's not the one. Don't force a title on her that she doesn't deserve. Men kill me with this! We need not get this confused because a man who gets the woman he wants is a happy camper from day one. If he puts in the work to get to know who she is and he still likes her, then he's pretty set. He'll go hard for this woman and he'll even challenge himself to be better for her benefit. That's the difference that finding the one makes and that's the feeling every man wants. We all want our unicorn woman and I say, if you work hard in life, you deserve her. Just be real about it, though.

DOES SHE FIT THE ROLE YOU NEED HER TO PLAY?

Today's relationships have feminist principles written all over them and that's not necessarily a good thing like many of us have been programmed to believe. I'm all for gender equality in the sense that a woman's value shouldn't equate to less than a man's value in any arena—professionally or personally. But I'm not of the mindset that my ideal woman should get comfortable playing the role I believe that a man should inherently play. What I mean is this, if you're stepping up to the plate to guide, provide and protect her, then she must step back to allow you to do that. The guide part would be critical, because if she's a western minded woman she may not know how let you be the man so you must be willing to show her how this benefits her life and your family. If you stepping up means she gets competitive about who's the leader, then you've got to consider that this may not be the woman for you. When a man is ready to lead and take on a family, the last thing he needs is a woman who is in conflict of him stepping up to do this. Men who work hard to provide for their families need a woman with a high sense of femininity to accompany and offset his high drive masculinity. If she wants to be the man, too then heads will bump and conflicts will escalate due to the high levels of testosterone present in both parties.

Many of today's women pat themselves on their backs for their ability to work full-time outside of the house while also maintaining their feminine touch at home, but many don't have a choice in the matter; overworking to pay bills with not much left in the tank when she gets home has become the standard for most educated American women. Society has now created ideals where women welcome doing it all professionally while also raising children- primarily on their own. Many of these women feel their biggest contribution is the income they get from working so hard. For many it is their biggest contribution because they themselves don't value the feminine role that women of old were known for. The woman that climbs any corporate ladder feels obligated to maintain that job because 1) she's driven to prove her worth in that arena and 2) she feels she can't rely on a man to take care of her if she doesn't work so hard. That ideal itself will create conflict in any relationship where the man has established himself as the leader of his household. Even if he makes two dollars to every dollar that she makes, she's still working hard for that dollar and she will demand to be respected by the weight of her financial contributions, too. A woman who has been conditioned to do it all with and without the help of a man will be reluctant to allow a man to lead because after doing it all herself, she now feels she doesn't need him for much. This is becoming common theology today; however, this isn't the kind of relationship or partnership I advocate for. I advocate for a man being a man and by doing so, he makes it easier for a woman to be a woman. We have to clear the clutter for each other to do our best work. It's counterproductive to hinder your partner's natural growth in their role. It's also counterproductive for a man to think that somehow he's going to recondition a masculine woman into a feminine wife.

Today there are legions of men who have been raised by independent-minded mothers. These men have subconsciously accepted this as what is normal and subsequently support their women playing more of a man's role because this is what they witnessed their mothers do. He has been unconsciously emasculated and subconsciously supports his woman's false masculine ego that maintains the idea that she can sustain herself without him. When a man has children with such a woman, he's also signing up to be pushed out of the child's life if the woman deems him no longer necessary. Men must know what kind of women they want in their corner because we're wrong when we think that all women want a man who is a provider or a leader. Some women want and need a man who is less masculine because they feel more in control and less obligated to his needs or demands. Listen, if you were raised by a single mother or around a culture of women who feel they don't need a man, you might find yourself attracted to women who only need you for sex and romantic holidays. You may not realize that's what your upbringing has conditioned you to accept, but sadly, for many men it is. They don't want a woman who is too dependent on them. They're afraid to be the man; afraid to lead and afraid to take the blame when things go wrong. These men need to be careful to know themselves and what they want before getting involved in relationships because independent women don't always support a man's rise from the bottom to the top for the fear that his pay scale may actually demand a woman who is more feminine by nature and he leave her. This kind of woman may suppress your greatness so you must know the role you want your woman to play in your life in advance. That means you must have a plan or a vision for your life in advance, too.

LEADER OF THE FAMILY

A sad truth today is that many men don't want to be the leader in the family so allowing a "strong" woman to lead takes pressure off of his shoulders. What the man just doesn't understand is that over time this woman will become hardened from the rigors of playing both roles and is more prone to sickness and disease from the additional amount of stress that she bears. I won't even go into the statistics of lifestyle diseases that plague our hard working women because many men are so incapable of stepping up to the plate to carry more of the weight so that their women don't have to go out to work 8-12 hours five days of the week for someone else. We've normalized this dysfunctionality and have accepted it as law when just 60 years ago you'd be hard pressed to find many women who worked outside of their homes and communities. This form of gender neutrality always creates confusion in the mind and heart because this woman will be in conflict about who to be loyal to- the job that pays her or the husband that needs her to work at the job? Men must become the leaders who can take nothing and make something out of it that benefits the whole family. This is what women once chose men for.

I hope you see why it's so important for man to have purpose and a plan before he finds himself in serious relationships or even in marriage. It's even more important as a man to pair yourself with a woman who is in agreement with your plan and can add to it to make it more achievable. Today's feminist minded women will disagree about men being leaders of the family, but they can't disagree with the fact that single mothers, regardless of their social status, are perhaps the most stressed out segment of the population. African American single mothers are also some of the sickest women and the sickness is not just physical, but also mental and emotional. She needs a break and she can't get one because many men do not want to lead nor to be held accountable. As a leader of your family unit, your wife has to be a contributor, but your contributions alone should be valued so much that she'll never feel that she's better off without you. If she feels this way, don't marry her until she realizes that she is indeed better off with you! You shouldn't have to convince her either. You should just be able to do the work that makes such a difference in her life that she notices it immediately. These are social issues we face in America and in the black community today that makes it so much harder for marriages to prosper. But I feel it's nothing that a man with a strong sense of purpose and the gusto to execute his vision can't overcome. Strong women will either need to accept your love and leadership as a package deal or continue being independent—without you.

INDIGENOUS RELATIONSHIPS

There are a lot of people who come from indigenous roots they can't trace. Today's relationships are like GMO (Genetically Modified Organisms) that are short circuiting. A lot of what it takes to be together successfully is still within us all, but society has waged a media-fueled war against the institution of family. And it's been done in its separate categories for men, women, and children throughout their life cycles. The media is all in your head about what to think about practically every facet of your life and your relationships. The ones who manage to survive the brainwashing are undoubtedly still connected to their indigenous instinct that drives them to a more simplified, role specific, co-independent lifestyle. This isn't an easy position to play these days because we live in a society where people from all over the world with different roots and cultures are constantly absorbing from mainstream media. For the most part, civilization and society has already killed off most indigenous cultures. With their death also came a lot of basic things about how men and women govern themselves. It's sad that we're at such a loss, but we must pick up the pieces to reestablishing stronger family units that don't lose their way every other generation or so. It's hard to say that one way fits all, but it's easy to say that the way things are today for the common man shows that this way doesn't work. It's our choice to continue dysfunction or forge a new path.

Amongst wealthy families, there rarely are power clashes between men and women, because the men are established as leaders in their families, and they are respected as such. Every kind of arrangement exists, but the ones where men and women chose to be with each other as a part of communities and villages seem to have always thrived. Men and women work together to build and expand their own progeny within small or large groups. We are both innately incredibly fond of the roles we play for each other. It's obvious to see across all cultures that boys and girls typically become attracted to each other within the same age ranges. The love energy vibrates so much higher when consistent interdependency roles are created and maintained. Marriage means different things in different cultures, and many ancient marriages had men marrying multiple women. But sex and physical attraction transcends marriage. You don't have to be married to want love and affection from someone.

All humans across the globe do the same things—we eat, sleep, have sex and labor. We work our specific position within a unit for our survival, and we enjoy our existence here. Our role is usually defined by the needs of our communities and the aptitude of our talents. Men who can give more rise to the top in value to their communities when they give more. Those men are relied upon to lead and create others like themselves among men in their community because the community is advanced by the doings of the super talented and hard working.

Indigenous relationships aren't necessarily about indigenous-styled relationships that men form with women, but more so the relationship that man forms with his environment. Men and women will go in the direction of where the food and shelter comes from. We are basic in design, but modernization has given us sophistication that implies that we need more than the basics to be happy. That's a complicated lie that we believed and look how it's complicated our male-female relationships. We don't know how to look for the basics in life anymore. We need the over the top solutions to everything. We're with the wrong people for the wrong reasons and we're unhappy. We don't value each other as much anymore because we live in an individualistic society that discourages communal living or communal anything. We have to relearn the basics of living and then the basics of partnering to win again in life.

RECOGNIZING COMPATIBILITY

Many men have already created soul ties and have had children with women who are opposed to their direction in life. This will require effective lifestyle management. The goal is to alleviate yourself from the stress and baggage of past mistakes by completely removing yourself from dysfunctional relationships. The goal is not to get someone to acquiesce to what you want, but rather to walk away from that kind of situation with humility and accountability because you know this is not a good fit for you.

It's important to immediately recognize whether you're compatible with a woman or not. Some practicing Jews marry Christians, but most don't because they value marrying someone of the same faith as them. Most people committed to a lifestyle will prefer to marry someone else who also shares the same lifestyle. This is the standard, not the exception. A severe case of strong feelings can sometimes confuse you into thinking you're compatible with someone who isn't a good match for you. Premature good sex can also confuse things. Lucky for most people blinded by hormones, there's a thing called time. Some people hit their heads and are asleep for years in dysfunctional relationships before they realize their incompatibility. When you finally snap out of it, you have no choice but to be responsible for your own ignorance. Pace yourself in new courtships and remember that men can be very blind to incompatibility when a woman is beautiful. So don't fall for it.

A good physical connection has high priority in the brain of any person. That response is a part of the brain that has been with humans throughout our physical development and evolution. A strong sexual connection has the power to propel men and women to become as one with each other. When you unlock the sexual healing secrets of love-making, you can grow incredibly strong relationships that transmute sexual energy into spiritual bliss. In the right environment, people will give up on habits and lifestyle customs to be with someone where an intense physical connection can be maintained over a long- term timeframe. There is artistry in lovemaking, and every woman is looking for a good artist.

This certainly isn't all that goes into compatibility, but it's a very strong component. We allowed politics and religion to make us asexual and now we want back our freedom to love. We've come to want power and social status more than we want to free ourselves in sexual bliss. This is so sad. And I'm not saying sexual compatibility is everything, but it goes hand in hand with attraction so it is indeed a big deal. When a man has become more than just a sexual object to a woman, he can attract women from a wider selection pool. Evolved men must choose women they are both attracted to and in agreement with; not one or the other.

Compatibility is simple. Find what you have in common and accentuate it. It'll be nice if you're both from the same place and have the same cultural background, but if not, there'll still be things that you have in common regardless of your differences. I talk about the need to for lifestyle compatibility and perhaps I say this because I'm so different. I'd love one day to live off the grid somewhere where I can't be texted or emailed so I know I'll need a woman who is will still be happy with me when I get to that place. Compatibility is sometimes short lived- when people pretend to be what you want until it no longer serves them. Your authenticity should be able to repel these kinds of women from your midst.

THE IDEAL ROLE OF A MAN

I'm clear that women aren't the way they used to be, but neither are men. Since the feminist movement has gone mainstream, divorce rates are up; single mom parenting is up, breast cancer rates are up; infertility in women is up, and a variety of other health ailments women face are now at all-time highs. If you ask me, men aren't protecting women the way they should be if in just 50 years we've allowed all this to happen to our women in the name of women's liberation. With more rights, the burden on women has increased dramatically, and it's quite obvious based on the widespread results that it hasn't helped to build stronger families. This is where men should look for opportunities to rise to the occasion and provide a better way for the women in his life.

The better attuned you are with your purpose and your role in life, the better your relationships will be with the opposite sex. Women will know what you're here to do and they will also know they benefit tremendously when you are purpose orientated in life. Today's modern world has redefined what a man is and how a man behaves in society. Most of us are programmed to behave how society wants us to function. Hard labor birth, daycare, pre-schooling, k-12, college or work. If your father sent you through this social conditioning, this is a major reason why many don't understand their role today.

A man should be free! The hardest part of life are the young and tender ages where your parents guard you for survival, but beyond that you're free to create in this world as you are called to. Instead of this, we've been given another form of lifestyle that serves the purpose of continuing the divide among the so called rich and the so called poor.

We were born to be free and man is the epitome of freedom. When a man is single and unattached, he is free to do and create in abundance without the feeling of responsibility to his offspring. This is where a man finds himself and most of today's young men are robbed of this. They were instead sold a life hyper masculinity and chauvinism; athletic dominance, hyper aggression and/or competitive academia. All of these paths are manufactured to shuffle you down, decreasing your likelihood of finding your true self and your purpose.

The modern world as we know it has emasculated men in ways that some of us are completely unaware of. You can't tell a woman you wear the pants in the house anymore because she now wears pants, too. But just as recently as 60 years ago, women didn't wear pants at all. You can't tell a woman that you provide food on the table because you don't know how to grow any food, all you know how to do is work for money to buy it. You can't fully protect your woman and children because for eight-ten hours of the day, you're off working for another man while your woman and children are at risk in this crazy world we live in. If your wife or children took sick, all you know how to do is take them to the hospital because you have no training on how to heal them, and you don't know many real healers who could actually help you. You can't build a house and maintain it so you hire someone else to do it. You and most other men in this modern world have no tangible survival skills that are needed to exist on this earth. Most of us are dependent, and we only see what's in front of us like electricity and running water. We're trained to think and believe that the way things are right now is the way they will always be and, therefore, we remain dependent on others who profit off providing us with resources we need because right now we see no other means to make it. We're dependent on stores, dependent on the government, the police, the hospitals, schools, etc. We send our children to get educated by a system that puts them in debt and takes away ownership from them. We no longer build for ourselves, and most men today don't understand that these were all invaluable skills that all men once needed to build families, communities, and get the girl. Now a superficial sense of dominance created from having money is how we assert ourselves as being the man while we lack the real skills that have defined men for thousands of years.

Pat yourself on the back for being born in a time where a man is less than a man!

Yet still, we are still instinctively the same as our ancestors. We're just as much of an animal as any other animal; we just have more control over the elements than they do. We're still driven by our will to survive in nature; still in need of the love of a woman, and we're still driven by sex to reproduce and build family units. Many of our human instincts have been bred out of us, but some of us are still connected to them. They say for most animals captured out of the wild and enslaved into zoos and circuses; it takes at least four generations to breed the wild out of them. Essentially meaning it took four generations of being bred in captivity for that lion you see at the zoo not to want to kill everything in sight. The lions you see there and their fore parents were born and raised in cages, so they're accustomed to the lifestyle of being a slave in a cage. They don't hunt like they're supposed to do. They're not in their natural habitat and aren't challenged by their natural enemies to maintain their strength and dominance. They don't even mate like they would normally do in the wild. They've been domesticated to play a role in a system that earns the zoo and circus operators profit. Don't be zoo man.

NATURAL MAN

We've been watered down and diluted to be less of the natural man we are instinctively designed to be. We've allowed the less talented, corporate-minded men to rise above us, the natural man. We can't protect ourselves like we're supposed to anymore because we live under a microscope. Our biggest show of strength is when commanded to by another man in what they call a military to go fight for resources that don't benefit the whole. We're not protecting our women and children at the home level like we should be. We allow all kinds of negative influences to come into our homes and affect our behavioral patterns. We don't form and build communities anymore; what we do is buy manufactured homes and live amongst each other in suburbs while largely remaining isolated from each other and unconnected. We call the police when we feel threatened instead of banding together to fight against injustice.

Everything has changed and if you pay attention, the biggest change factor is how men identify themselves with their roles in today's world. We're doing less and allowing people to govern us like children. The results are piss poor, yet we've somehow been convinced that we will be OK if we just made more money. Overall, the average man behaves powerlessly, even if he has the look of a big or strong man. All these things we allow go against the natural design of men, and because no one has ever told us what men really are, many of us remain in these boxes we've been placed in. It's such a simple concept that many will misunderstand the message here. We've been taught to focus on the obstacles that sometimes we never get past. We fear what would happen if were to truly live free and fear in the hearts of men the beginning of the deterioration of the soul of man. You say that you perhaps don't know how to be a natural man, but its 2016, you can learn to be who and whatever you want to be. You don't have to remain a captive of a lifestyle that doesn't enhance your existence.

Look at all these natural functioning's of men and women that have changed so much in such a short period of time. For the majority of anyone reading this, you probably fall into many of these categories. I know I do. But the animal in me is driving me to be a real man again; one who is free from the boxes others try to put him in. I've always been ostracized for my desires to break away from society and live in the wild, but the wild isn't even the wild anymore. And since surviving in nature is a skill that hasn't been passed down to me, it'll be something I have to learn if I want to do that. As for now, I have no choice but to strive to be in alignment with as much of my animalistic male instincts as possible right where I am, even though the environment suppresses it. Many of the ancient principles of being a man will be rejected by the modern man because his current lifestyle prevents him from being this kind of man. But the modern man bogged down by bills, child support, and sex should be listening to what is potentially an opportunity at freedom if you are willing to change the way you look at success for your life.

There's a lot of rewiring that needs to take place for men to evolve from where we currently are. Most of us have gotten used to the decaying state of manhood today, but I don't advocate getting too comfortable in today's climate. Definitions are changing fast, roles are becoming blurred, but you don't have to accept the trend. Men of distinction are men who are defined by how well they play their most critical roles. Many of today's mishaps in society are fueled by the re-appropriation of gender roles gone wrong. When men take a back seat and allow women to lead, they kill their instincts to play their natural role.

This book is for men who are humble enough to take the time to retreat from failing relationships to work on becoming a better man because you finally understand how valuable your role is. All you ever have to do is stop to analyze your moves, and if there are opportunities to do better for yourself, then you must take the necessary time needed to improve yourself and improve your chances of living a life of purpose and bliss. Never allow the mainstream or popular culture to determine your value. Men who are leaders should never allow their women to model themselves after dysfunctional role models. Seek to be the strong man who not only protects and provides but also prepares and guides his family.

THE NEW PECKING ORDER OF MANHOOD:

- **Define yourself & your contributions** – From the moment you're born, your life has been about unlocking your super powers. If as a child you weren't encouraged to find yourself, then you must stop everything you're doing now to find your true calling. Never put women or politics above this, no matter what! Practice self-disclosure with woman so they are never confused about who you are and what you stand for in life. Be so sure of who you are that others can help you, but they can never define you nor break you down.

- **The right woman**- The right woman will bolster your plans, your vision and will support you on your mission to fulfill your purpose in life. She will be your balance; she'll allow you to retreat inwards from the external world that you labor in. She will run the home you build and comfort you when you are challenged. When you know why you're here, you tell her and eliminate her if she's not in agreement with where you are headed in life. Her physical beauty and sexual intimacy can be a source of infinite inspiration and encouragement to you on your path.
- **Build**- Build and create everything you need for yourself and your family. Build the world where your children can be free from race based cultural warfare and modern day wage slavery. Build with your hands to influence your progeny that somethings you must go out and build from the bottom up without the help of others.
- **Grow**- Grow as much of your own food as you can; network with local farmers; become food independent; never allow the lack of finances or resources to prevent you from feeding your family. Never destroy nature because it is nature that provides us with all of our needs. Men must make the earth yield without destroying it. We can grow an abundance of food that can feed everyone on the planet.
- **Work**- Work towards your purpose tirelessly without the distractions of women and relationships. Align your work that with the needs of your family and your community—not corporate interest. Enterprise your skills; know the value of your craft, trade or skill set and use it for the purpose of securing resources for the whole. If you must work for someone else, work to become self-sustainable and return to working for your community.
- **Environment**- Connect first to the land you live on; understand its seasons, what grows there for food, the climate and the animals in the environment. Learn to thrive and produce off the land while

preserving the natural beauty of the land. Become a master of your environment and offer your mastery to your community.

- **Teach**- Teach your children your skills, teach them how preserve their environment, how to build, how to grow and the value of working together. Teach them the value of the lifestyle you lead (or desire to lead) and connect them to it so they can continue to thrive based on the survival skills they've learned. Teach them how to love themselves and their culture; and how to pursue their higher calling at a young age.

- **Prepare**- Prepare your land to provide resources for your community and family in case of emergency needs. Have a plan of where and how you will survive if and when things change. We can't expect things to remain the same and things usually get worse before they get better.

- **Protect**- Keep the women and children of your community in close proximity. Always be available to come to their aid. Teach them skills that will protect them in nature and in society when you are not around. Create inputs that keep you connected to them and their safety. Solve problems yourself without the need for law enforcers; create community-based resources that everyone can collectively maintain and share.

FATHERHOOD ISN'T FOR EVERY MAN

The lion's share of the responsibility is definitely for the man to carry, but that's just my opinion. Well, it's also based on the fact that most men are physically bigger and stronger than women for the purpose of doing the heavy lifting outside of the duties of child bearing. The way things are going these days, it's becoming clearer that many men would rather opt out of doing the family thing to make life easier and less stressful in a world where women and men don't stay together very long anymore. Opting to remain single may mean skipping out on children you fathered or not having children at all. Men in this predicament may feel completely defeated based on dysfunctional relationship history, but some are aware that the difference between them and their children's mother(s) in lifestyle and culture is sometimes big enough to neutralize their role in their children's lives. Basically, you can be a father paired with an opposing mother who will not get to effectively raise your sons or daughters to continue your work because the mother is in opposition to your purpose and cause in life. I hope that this isn't your fate with your children because it can be tormenting to raise children who will be hesitant to follow your lead because of their mothers' condescendence. You'd have to roll the dice on this and decide if how invested you'll be.

The old school proverb, "everything ain't for everybody," will always remain. Not every man in the history of mankind was meant to be a father, a husband or grow his own food. Some were here to play music, fight wars and cure disease. Don't force yourself to being what society expects of you because it seems like the right thing to do. Always seek out the path that allows you to be the truest to yourself. The right person to be is always you, not a carbon copy of society's ideal of a man.

A NATURAL SELECTION

When you take a position and stand by it, you'll end up yielding all of the benefits of that chosen position. Sometimes that includes losses, but if you're committed, you'll take the bitter with the sweet. If you don't get what you're looking for right away, dedicate more time to building you. Men must commit themselves to the lives they want to live regardless of the influence of women and children. We must never be separated or allow misunderstanding to grow between the women we partner with. We have to see where some of our point of views aren't natural, but are manufactured in order to sew dysfunction among us. We must begin to see through the façade of society to reconnect with basic instinctual living; a lifestyle where men and women lived happily together taking care of the earth and their basic needs.

A natural selection for you is an existence where you live a healthy and happy life for as long as you're called to live it for. There are a lot of ideals we get from society that are only as good as society is at its core. Civilizations always fail, and while moral decay tends to be the most recognizable trait of failing states and empires, so is the destruction of the environment. We see the moral decay in broad day, but wer rarely see the destruction and poisoning of the earth's natural resources. Societies go against the grain to provide you with a lifestyle that automatically guides people along the path of environmental and eventual self-destruction. The earth is our true mother and civilization as we know it is sophisticated exploitation of the earth and its natural resources. It's not natural and we all know it. But we stay put like good little boys because of fear based social conditioning. Throughout your lifetime living in today's world, it will continue to become evident that your life is being manipulated because you've been stripped of your natural programming to be free.

Most men aren't preparing for life after the matrix, but you should be because change is the only thing that's constant about life. To be the leader you need to be, you must make the best use of the information you have available to create more for all. When you are accountable to more than yourself and your decisions affect the livelihood of others, you are forced to become wiser about those decisions. We must become captains of our perspective ships and be able to analyze the now for insights of what the future holds for you. We live in a changing time where the global climate is changing so fast that every man will inevitably have to provide for himself or become slaves who work for genetically modified foods. The rebirth of man mandates that men be reconnected to the earth. All men can become masters of the basics of living to guide their families through foreseen and unforeseen tough times.

DON'T SETTLE FOR JUST ANYONE

A few years ago an old college friend of mine would take to Facebook to make posts about his unwillingness to settle for just anyone. He'd rant about the letdowns of the dating world and the struggles he had meeting women who may have been a good fit for someone else, but not for him. I considered him ultra-picky. And he admittedly was.

It'll be a couple years later before I fully realized how important it is for man not to settle for whoever is willing to give it up first. Much like most other animals, the male generally puts on some kind of performance or show of strength to sway a female to choose him over others. That's the pursuit, and men love the feeling that comes from preparing to be chosen. The evolved man loves it even more when the woman he is in pursuit of is not only physically attractive but also spiritually compatible. While physical attraction is the flame, spiritual or lifestyle compatibility is the glue that holds successful relationships together.

You truly cannot settle at this stage in the evolution of relationships. Especially not after taking a break and improving yourself. You don't settle, you choose someone who satisfies your wants and needs within the same cultural perspective as yours. You don't want a complete stranger who speaks another language unless you know for a fact that she wants what you want and can be supportive of you. The courtship process is so important to help you in your choosing process. You need time, but you also need to converse about the values and core beliefs that are important in the relationship you desire. A woman can easily could be your physical match, but share no common lifestyle standards with you. That wouldn't work very well, no matter how attracted you are to her.

THE FAMILY STARTS WITH YOU

Don't believe the hype of today. Women do need men. If you've learned anything from this book, it should be that your value as a man is infinite if you actually made it from boyhood to manhood. The more lessons you've received in life to prepare you to live in truth and with purpose, the more ready you may be to pursuit love. Once you know yourself and your worth, it'll become law to you to never endanger your progress with women who are in opposition to the lifestyle you strive towards. You won't try to save or convince a woman why she should be with you. You'll know she's for you and she'll know you're for her because the energy you give to her is authentically you and it attracts to you what you are. When a man is living his life with purpose, fulfilment comes out this lifestyle and a man can give that to his woman in the form physical love and affection. There are other things that a man will be, by default providing for the women of his tribe, but he can give intimate love and affection more freely once he has answered to his calling in life. This is the metaphor of going to heaven with seven virgins: you live a life of honor and purpose and you will be rewarded with a woman who loves you because of who you are, not what she wants you to be. This is what a woman would want her any husband- for him to have fulfilment of purpose so she can be loved by someone who is not lacking or depressed, but is filled with love, experience and know how.

By know we all should know that the right woman is critical to your success. The timing that she comes along must be when she will not be a distraction from your healing or knowing of self. Since this isn't a perfect world, on your relationship break, you must work on healing and improving yourself before you even think about relationships again. Set a goal for yourself and stay focused on it without diverting your attention to women until you reach that goal. You must emulate success and never take your focus off of you answering to your highest calling in life. The happiest and truest love you'll find as a man will be in the woman who awaits you after your journey to your higher self. You won't have to fight and argue with her, if there are no fights and arguments happening within you. She will meet you where your preparation left you. She will help you accomplish more if you're still on your path and she will help you experience endless bliss and passion if you've answered your calling and are ready for a family.

This whole book is a call for men to answer to the calling of their true selves. Peaceful and blissful love awaits you after you've answered that calling and started your journey. In today's world, men of all ages who know they are not happy with where they are in life need to stop and begin to focus on what they need to be doing to be happy and true to their calling. This is the man who will bring back loving families that will become villages of peace that nurture children filled with love and dedication to their purpose. Selah.

ABOUT THE AUTHOR &
WAYS TO CONNECT

Social Media

Instagram: @IAMNAKADA | Twitter: @IAMNAKADA |
Facebook: @heartonbreak

Websites

www.heartonbreak.com
www.iamnakada.com

Titles by Nakada

5 Winning Relationship Strategies for Men: Five insightful strategies for
men who are serious about qualifying and disqualifying women without
getting sexually involved. Available on Heartonbreak.com.

Attend my Workshops & Events

My second wild foray into sexual promiscuity in my late twenties with
the use of undeveloped tantric sex moves lead to unhealthy soul ties
and multiple pregnancies with women who matched my low vibration
at the time. I was naïve and immature and I could hear my father
telling me this isn't what I taught you. Chaos ensued and as I crashed
and burned, I was forced to pick up the pieces. I was forced to look at

everything from my past that contributed to my state of unhappiness. And because I had done better before, with time I was able to see where I errored.

I ended up asking myself some critical questions:

- Why did I get caught up?
- If I knew better why didn't I do better?
- Why didn't I wear a condom?
- Is my manhood authentic?
- Was I crying out for love?
- Why did I put others before my purpose?
- What made me think I could change women?
- Why did I try to control things?
- Am I a "real man?"

I got answers to all these questions when I decided to block out all the distractions and focus only on answering to my highest calling. It didn't come all at once, b/c there were soft spots from the past that I didn't want to explore, but I had to face my truth- no matter how bad it made me look and feel.

I am committed to helping every man who was never encouraged to find himself; every man who had children with women they quickly fell out of love with; every man who needs to learn to accept himself and pursue his purpose above all other things in life; every father who wants to leave a legacy for his children and his family. We must rebuild our families and men must once again know how important their role is in this process. Let's build.

Email heartonbreak@gmail.com if you are interested in workshops and events in your city, personal or group coaching.

89795628R00091

Made in the USA
Middletown, DE
18 September 2018